TRIVIA PURSUIT

TRIVIA PURSUIT

How Showbiz Values Are Corrupting the News

Knowlton Nash

M&S

Canadian Cataloguing in Publication Data

Nash, Knowlton
    Trivia pursuit

ISBN 0-7710-6752-6

1. Journalism.   2. Journalism – Objectivity.   3. Journalism – Social aspects.   I. Title.

PN4731.N37   1998   070.4   C98-931179-1

We acknowledge the financial support of the Government of Canada through the Book Publishing Industry Development Program for our publishing activities. We further acknowledge the support of the Canada Council for the Arts and the Ontario Arts Council for our publishing program.

Typeset in Minion by M&S, Toronto
Printed and bound in Canada

McClelland & Stewart Inc.
The Canadian Publishers
481 University Avenue
Toronto, Ontario
M5G 2E9

1 2 3 4 5   02 01 00 99 98

To the foot soldiers of journalism
who tell it like it is

Contents

Introduction

Writing this book has been a voyage of discovery for me, exploring where journalism has been, where it is now, and, most important of all, where it is going.

I've had a half-century love affair with the news, and the battle for better journalism, especially TV journalism, has been my particular lodestar as a foreign correspondent, a news executive, an anchor for the CBC's *The National*, and a senior correspondent. Writing for magazines and newspapers and broadcasting for radio and television has given me a broad perspective on this business of journalism.

It's a beautiful business, and one I honour, but it's a business in trouble because of its current obsession with immediacy, with the pursuit of trivia, with entertainment and gossip. The challenge for journalists is not only to recognize the public's thirst for diversion, but also to recognize its need for substance in the news. The answer is to make the important interesting, not to make the merely interesting seem important. The task for those of us in the news business is to strive continually to provide a fair reflection of reality so people can understand and cope.

There is much to be proud of in the history of journalism and not a little to be ashamed of. As an instrument of democracy, journalism has played a critical role over the centuries in the struggle of people to free their societies from autocratic Tudor kings and communist dictators alike. It has become the most powerful product in the world and one of the most profitable. The arrival of mass communication induced the biggest change in the history of human awareness. But journalism also has catered to sensationalism, oversimplification, and misunderstanding.

In the business of news, there is a tendency to species affinity, with journalists publicly defending any and all news colleagues no matter our private reservations. But our role is too important to society as a whole for us to evade rigorous self-examination.

For centuries there has been a continuing battle within journalism between those who believe its role is to educate and those who believe it's to entertain. In the ebb and flow of that battle, we now show signs of returning to the values of the Yellow Press of a century ago, which fed readers a steady diet of scandal and sleaze. This regression is spurred by greed, by fear, by miscalculation, and by perversion of the new technology, and is signalled by the sensationalism of the tabloid press beginning to leak into the mainstream media and pour onto the Internet. Supermarket tabloids are sometimes fun to read, but, drenched in triviality as they are, they are for entertainment, not information or knowledge.

From O. J. Simpson's murder trial to Princess Diana's death to the sex allegations against U.S. President Bill Clinton, the media's sensationalist overkill has seriously damaged their credibility. Ferocious competition for audience, fanned by the tabloids, the Internet, and television's twenty-four-hour news channels, has goaded mainstream journalism into sometimes abandoning time-honoured values.

The media's premature adjudication of the sex accusations against Clinton made in early 1998 represented the most flagrant desertion of journalistic professionalism in recent memory. Wild, unverified, anonymous accusations were suddenly elevated to the status of legitimate news as the networks and newspapers rushed to judgement. In the frenzy of the breaking story, the principle of double-checking facts simply went out the window in all but a handful of news outlets. It was a sorry spectacle, as the wall between tabloid sensationalism and mainstream journalism crumbled.

"The type of news essential to an increase in circulation, to an increase in advertising . . . was essentially that which catered to excitement," said Canadian communications philosopher Harold Innis. The chase after bigger profits, Innis feared, inevitably led the news media into cheaper journalism. Exciting news may be profitable, but it can have damaging consequences. When sensationalism dominates the news, transitory, popular passion can dominate reason, and political mischief is allowed to go unchecked when the public is ignorant of or indifferent to serious issues. Journalism that splashes in sensationalism and promotes illusions while minimizing perplexing issues and sour truths about today's world may profoundly damage our democratic society. "Knowledge is power," English philosopher and statesman Sir Francis Bacon said four centuries ago, and it is the responsibility of journalism to supply serious news prepared as interestingly as possible to reach as many people as possible without distorting or cheapening the substance.

Readers, listeners, and viewers who are disengaged and not inspired to seek out serious journalism may be victims of media theatrics, but they also have to take responsibility for their lack of awareness. Their knowledge is their power, and they must reach out for that knowledge.

It is not only the editorial hazards of the present that concern me, but also the technological challenges of the future. Technology has always had and will continue to have a fundamental effect on the kind of news we read, hear, and see. At the end of the twentieth century, the way we communicate is undergoing a technological revolution called the Internet. Frankly, I sympathize with Eugene Patterson, the president of Florida's *St. Petersburg Times*, who said, "I'm sure that this Internet is important. I'm sure that something is happening. But I'll be goddamned if I know what it is!"

Technology is essentially a neutral force; whether it has positive or negative effects depends on what we do with it. I believe that right now we are dumbing down society through misuse of the new communications technology and through the erratic responses to it on the part of much of the media. Those responses are fed by the mistaken perception that we all have an insatiable desire to run away from reality. A growing number of publishers and broadcasters are going "down market," convinced that entertaining diversions are more palatable and more profitable than serious news.

If media success is measured only by the size of the audience, as it most often is these days, the most successful journalism is that which caters to the lowest common denominator. To wit, with a circulation of nearly 3 million, the weekly supermarket gossip sheet *National Enquirer* is the biggest-selling newspaper in the United States. Its equivalents in Britain, the *Sun*, with nearly 4 million daily circulation, and the weekly *News of the World*, which has had a high of 8.5 million, have larger circulations than any other British papers; and Germany's lively *Bild Zeitung*, with a 5.5 million circulation, outsells all other German papers. While not nearly as flamboyant as its Western counterparts, the biggest-selling paper in Russia, *Argumenti i Fakti* (Arguments and Facts), is a breezy mix of short, abrasive articles, celebrity interviews, advice columns on sex, and do-it-yourself projects. Latin America has some of the world's most shamelessly garish newspapers; in Managua, Nicaragua, in the spring of 1988, a new daily paper, *El Mercurio*, proudly called itself "the yellowest of the yellow."

The contrast between tawdry and quality newspapers is nowhere more vivid than in London, which has some of the world's best and worst newspapers. The daily tabloids the *Sun*, the *Mirror*, the *Star*, and the once influential *Daily Express* and *Daily Mail* contrast sharply with the high-quality journalism of the *Daily Telegraph*, the *Times*, the *Guardian*, the *Financial Times*, and the *Independent*. Altogether, these dailies make London the most exciting and enriching newspaper city in the world and the greatest battlefield of news as education versus news as entertainment.

American columnist Walter Lippmann once said that reporting is "the last refuge of the vaguely talented." As we enter a new millennium, journalists must use their "vague talents" to provide Canadians with a wake-up call to reality. In the short run, I confess I'm a pessimist about that happening, but in the long run, I'm an optimist. I believe that, in time, we will overcome our bewitchment by sensationalism.

Journalists may well discover that quality pays.

Through more than five decades, journalism has taken me on a journey of joys, giving me a front-row seat at history's passing parade. I owe much to many for making the journey professionally fulfilling, personally enriching, and frequently rollicking. If I expect a lot from the news media, it's because what we do in journalism has enormous importance and impact, even if most of us don't take ourselves too seriously. But when we go wrong, it hurts. This book is a personal cry of pain that we are in danger of going wrong in a serious way.

1

Dumbing Down the News

"**R**ead all about it! Murder in the streets! Read all about it! Vicious murder in the streets!"

My twelve-year-old voice crackled with urgency as I began a love affair with journalism nearly six decades ago by misleading the public. I was a newsboy selling papers on a Toronto street corner, and while my cries about murder in the streets sold lots of papers, what I didn't say was that the murder was in Los Angeles, not Toronto, a fact that my customers found out on page two.

Every day after school, I'd rush to the corner of Bathurst and Eglinton to tear open my bundles of the *Toronto Star* and the now defunct Toronto *Telegram*. I still can smell the deep sweetness of the fresh ink as the papers tumbled out. I'd quickly search for some exciting story that I could use to attract attention. My shouted exaggerations served the same purpose as the headlines I later saw chalked on newsstand blackboards in London screaming out overwrought tidbits of the Fleet Street press. In both cases, the hyperbole sold papers, making millions for the press barons and for me, selling the *Star* and the *Tely* at three cents a paper, loading the pockets of my short pants with so many coins, they almost fell off. Clearly, hyping the news paid off for me, as well as the press barons.

It's been paying off for centuries. Shouting the news has been a tradition since children hollered out sensationalist headlines to sell their papers on the streets of London in the early 1600s. The English writer W. T. Stead in the late 1800s offered a rationale for the practice: "It is the thing you shout that will command attention . . . and compel the people to ask, 'What is it all about?'"

Although I am now chagrined at my deception of the public, it just never occurred to my juvenile mind that crying out misleading headlines was wrong. I was entranced at the time by the excitement of news, which for me was personified by the frenzied voice of the hugely popular New York gossip columnist Walter Winchell barking out the news on Sunday-night radio to the beat of a pulsating dot-dash telegraph key. It would be years before I was more influenced by the widely respected Washington columnist and journalistic philosopher Walter Lippmann and decades before Walter Cronkite set for me the standard for television journalism. Through my teenage years and into adulthood, I grew up with the three Walters. They – Winchell, Lippmann, and Cronkite – taught me valuable lessons of what to do and what not to do as a journalist.

But at the beginning, it was the exhibitionist journalism of Winchell that seized my attention. A decade after my newsboy days, when I was a British United Press (BUP) reporter covering a Doukhobor demonstration in Krestova, British Columbia, I was sent to report on a group of teenaged Doukhobors who were marching nude, accompanied by several farm horses, along a highway to protest government interference in their lives. My first lead in the story simply recounted the facts: "Krestova, B.C. (BUP) – Led by a pretty young girl, forty naked teen-age Doukhobors marched in protest here today." The reporter for the opposition, the Canadian Press, had a more exciting lead: "Led by a blonde beauty, forty teen-age Doukhobors stripped in a protest march here today."

Not to be outdone, I rewrote my story, changing the colour of the "beauty's" hair and putting her atop one of the horses. The new lead was "Krestova, B.C. (BUP) – Led by a bare-breasted, raven-haired beauty straddling a frisky horse, forty naked teen-age Doukhobors marched in protest here today." Walter Winchell couldn't have done it better, and my story got front-page treatment across the country. I easily ignored a momentary pang of guilt at the distortion of the story as congratulatory messages poured in for beating the opposition so thoroughly.

When I started out, I had a romantic notion of the news business. I was thrilled by the derring-do of reporters in Hollywood movies of the late 1930s and early 1940s, such as Joel McCrea as an innocent but determined reporter trying to stop the Second World War in *Foreign Correspondent* (1940), or Clark Gable in *Too Hot to Handle* (1938) as a hard-working, hard-drinking, vagabond newsreel cameraman filming the Japan–China war of the late 1930s. At the same time, I raced through the pages of *I Found No Peace*, which chronicled the globe-trotting adventures of a United Press (UP) foreign correspondent by the name of Webb Miller. In my teenage wonder, Miller's journalistic exploits in distant, exotic lands catapulted me into a lifelong passion for the news. It was the irresistible fascination of history on the run.

Journalism was an exciting game in a magic world, and I was determined to be a participant. It was fun, pure and simple.

And that sense of fun has persisted through more than half a century of earning my living as a journalist.

During those years, I've learned that news is far more than an exciting game. The critical lesson is that the news must be made as interesting as possible, but never at the cost of distortion. Sadly, that's not happening. With the trend of using shrieking headlines, "sound bites," slogans, and modified truths, the contemporary media increasingly put more emphasis on the interesting and less on the important. Image is triumphing over reality in a kind of Gresham's Law of bad news driving out good.

Media critic Neil Postman has noted that the real danger to democracy is not so much government censorship of the form George Orwell envisioned in *1984*, but rather the trivialization of culture and preoccupation with, as Postman put it, "entertaining ourselves to death" that Aldous Huxley predicted in *Brave New World*. Postman's comment has particular relevance to television, which is where most people today get their news.

Television news, said famed American diplomat and historian George Kennan, too often offers "floating, disjointed visual glimpses of reality, flickering on and off the screen." Consumer critic Ralph Nader has said TV news is "something that jerks your head up every ten seconds."

Television news is more susceptible to the values of the entertainment world than newspapers are because TV is essentially part of that world. As a result, many producers assume that people prefer fantasy to fact, find illusion more comfortable than reality. Much of the news business is becoming showbiz as the gap shrinks between *Oprah* or *Geraldo* and network newscasts. ABC network correspondent Diane Sawyer, who is paid about $7 million a year, exemplified the shrinking of the gap in her prime-time interview with the mistress of mega-builder Donald Trump when she asked her, "Was it the best sex you ever had?" At the height of the media frenzy over the allegations of sexual impropriety involving U.S. President Bill Clinton and White House intern Monica Lewinsky in early 1998, CNN anchor Judy Woodruff began a newscast by saying, "If men are from Mars and women from Venus, how does that factor in the president's problems?" The idea of the journalist as teacher is clearly losing out to the journalist as entertainer.

On a late-spring day in 1997, the U.S. Supreme Court ordered President Bill Clinton to answer questions from the lawyers for Paula Jones, who accused him of sexual misbehaviour and who said he had "distinguishing characteristics" in the presidential genital area, including a bent penis. The president's lawyer responded in a CBS *Face the Nation* program that "in terms of size, shape, direction . . . the president is a normal man. There are no blemishes, there are no moles, there are no growths." On the same day that the Supreme Court ruled Clinton must testify in the case, Russian President Boris Yeltsin declared that Russia would no longer point its missiles at Washington and New York, thus ending the long-time threat of the nuclear annihilation of millions of Americans. Most U.S. newspapers gave more prominence to the travails of Clinton's penis than to the removal of the Russian nuclear threat.

Eight months later, it got worse with the fevered media coverage of Clinton and Monica Lewinsky. Never before in modern times had the mainstream news media gone so awry in reporting salacious innuendo, second- and third-hand hearsay, anonymous leaks, single-source allegations, and rampant speculation. "I think a lot of us are in uncharted territory here," said CBS News president Andrew Heyward.

The real issues in the case were totally obscured by the journalists' focus on sensationalism and the blurring of the distinction between gossip and hard fact. In the first days of the story, there was speculation – and in some cases flat assertions, such as those made by ABC's Sam Donaldson – that Clinton would be out of office within a week. Rivalling the tabloids, the mainstream news media reported on adultery, oral sex, presidential semen on a blue dress, secret White House trysts, telephone sex, and accusations that Hillary Clinton was frigid. The *New York Post* headline trumpeted, "Hundreds of Clinton Sex Partners." Little of what was written was based on confirmed information. Suddenly the media was awash in high-level sex. In Britain, the tabloid *Daily Mirror* headlined the story "Fornigate" while the *Sun* front page called it "Zippergate." In Canada, the *Toronto Sun*'s headline read, "Hillary's Not Into Sex, Says Clinton Buddy." In Managua, Nicaragua, *El Nuevo Diario*'s headline banner read, "Is Clinton a Sex Maniac?"

Clinton could be forgiven if he agreed with Oscar Wilde, whose widely reported homosexual exploits ruined him, when he said, "In the old days, men had the rack. Now, they have the press."

Hundreds of Internet sites sprung up in the first week of the story. One Web site offered nude photos of Lewinsky, and *Penthouse Magazine* offered her $2 million to pose naked. In the seven days after the Clinton–Lewinsky story broke, the three big U.S. TV networks carried 124 evening news stories on the scandal, according to a Reuters news agency tabulation. During those first seven days, on average the Clinton–Lewinsky story took 67 per cent of the airtime that the three U.S. networks allocate to news. In the same time period, the historic visit of the Pope to Cuba got 11 per cent of the network news time.

By the time I had been in the business of journalism for a few years, my editors had drummed into my head the rule "Get it first, but first get it right!" It was a holy mantra, but it seemed to be abandoned by many journalists covering the Clinton–Lewinsky story in its early stages. The editors who splashed the story on their front pages and newscasts were uneasy about the absence of verification in some cases, but felt they had to use the story because their competitors were using it. And so the high ideals of journalism were subverted at least momentarily by cheap practices, as competitiveness got in the way of media integrity. Maybe it would be helpful to return to the occasional practice of nineteenth-century newspapers, which, in reporting a story not fully confirmed, would carry a subheading "Probably Not True" or "Important If True."

"It is one of the most sorry chapters in American journalism," says Marvin Kalb, former network correspondent and now director of Harvard University's Center on the Press, Politics and Public Policy. "We have a storm of half-baked, unsubstantiated gossip, innuendo, and rumour coming out with very little hard facts. We live in a new journalistic culture."

Kalb's lament echoes a comment made a century and a half ago by the French politician and writer Alexis de Tocqueville. In 1835, following a visit to the United States, he noted, "The journalists of the United States possess a vulgar turn of mind. The American journalist abandons principles to assail the characters of individuals, to track them into private life and disclose all their weaknesses and vices."

Shortly before the Clinton–Lewinsky story broke, a survey taken and published by *Editor and Publisher*, the Bible of the North American news industry, shared at least some of de Tocqueville's concerns. The survey showed that nearly half of the editors in the United States think press coverage is shallow and inadequate; slightly more than half believe the press is too cynical; and two-thirds say there is too much focus on personalities. The Pew Research Center for the People and the Press in a 1988 survey on media credibility reported that 63 per cent of Americans it surveyed believed news stories are often inaccurate.

The flip side of the sensationalized mainstream media coverage of the Clinton–Lewinsky story was the minimal front-page coverage given to critically important stories: the beginning of the Iraq–U.S. confrontation over weapons inspections; the economic crisis in Asia; growing Israeli–Palestinian tensions; the British prime minister's visit to the United States; and the Pope's historic visit to Cuba. These stories were relegated to secondary coverage to make way for the presidential sex reports.

After a week or so of revelling in titillating stories, the U.S. media began to turn on itself. *Time* magazine managing editor Walter Isaacson commented, "It does feel, when you look at this whole scenario, we must have lost our minds. This has gotten out of control." Two-time Pulitzer Prize-winner and veteran *Des Moines Register* Washington bureau manager James V. Risser echoed that comment: "Some of the media are out of control in covering this story." CNN aired a discussion on the journalists' recycling of gossip under the title "Media Madness?"

The three U.S. network anchors – Dan Rather, Peter Jennings, and Tom Brokaw – all adopted a *mea culpa* attitude on the story. "It's about circulation and ratings," Rather said. "It's about competitive pressures." In other words, the devil made them do it.

Washington correspondents at least could laugh at themselves. At their 1998 annual Gridiron Dinner, where, as happens
at Ottawa's Parliamentary Press Gallery annual dinner, the
journalists roast the politicians, this time the journalists roasted
themselves. To the tune of "Anything Goes," reporters wearing
trench coats and waving notebooks sang, "So when reporting
stuff salacious and even outright fallacious, just hold your nose.
Anything goes." The chorus ended with "God how we love it –
wallowing deep in muck and slime. Lurid tales? We're not above
it. Sex sells papers every time."

At the spring 1998 meeting of the American Society of
Newspaper Editors, its president, Sandra Mims Rowe, editor
of the Portland *Oregonian*, said, "If this is a time when the
destructiveness and tawdriness of mass media hang like a curse
over even the best-intentioned newspaper editors, it is also a
time when changing values and new media players should
prompt us to seek higher ground."

The public's reaction to all the allegations against Clinton
was surprising. After the first two weeks of the story, polls
showed that Clinton's approval rating zoomed to an all-time
high of 73 per cent. A survey by the Media Studies Center of
the Freedom Forum Foundation in the United States revealed
that 68 per cent of people polled felt that the media were not
taking enough care to be sure of their facts; 60 per cent felt
that the media went too far in reporting the details; and 81 per
cent said that the media were more interested in attracting
bigger audiences than in getting to the bottom of the story.
After a week or so of lurid headlines, most of the mainstream
media began reacquainting themselves with their ethics and
standards, and coverage finally became somewhat less speculative and sensational.

Canadian reportage throughout the story was more subdued in both volume and graphic detail. Even so, an Angus Reid
poll found that two-thirds of people it surveyed accused the
media of sensationalism and one-third said they had boycotted
certain media because of the way reported stories such as the
Clinton White House sex scandal and the death of Princess
Diana were reported.

Historically, Canadian journalists have been less aggressive
in examining the private lives of political leaders. The break-
up of Pierre and Margaret Trudeau's marriage while he was
prime minister certainly got headlines, but the coverage was
restrained. So, too, was the later reporting on Trudeau's father-
ing of an out-of-wedlock child with a prominent senior political adviser. Earlier this century, it was widely known in Ottawa
that Sir Wilfrid Laurier had a mistress while he was prime minister, but the story never made the papers. Nor was Prime
Minister Mackenzie King's deep interest in prostitutes covered
in the media until long after his death.

Other sensational stories have been treated circumspectly
by Canadian reporters. There was widespread media coverage
of the notorious trials of Karla Homolka and her husband, Paul
Bernardo. Although the story involved sex games, rape, and
murder, coverage was relatively restrained, at least compared to
the U.S. media's reporting on the O. J. Simpson murder trial.
Partly, this is because of Canadian law that permits a judge to
bar reporting of the more horrendous details of a crime.
"Sensationalist cases in Canada are less sensational and less
likely to produce the circuses that marked several American trials in recent years," says Stuart Adam, vice-president (acade-
mic) of Ottawa's Carleton University and former director of the
Carleton School of Journalism.

The chance that, in time, the sex accusations against President Clinton might turn out to be true is used to justify the kind of cowboy coverage that a frenzied media inflicted on the public at the beginning of the scandal. Media credibility is the only thing that really matters, and it is seriously damaged by rush-to-judgement sensationalism, even if that sensationalism turns out to have been aimed in the right direction.

The difference between what the news media did with this story and what I did as a newsboy shouting misleading headlines is only a matter of degree. The real danger of the news media's focus on the trivial is that we dumb down society itself. In time, there will be hell to pay, because an ill-informed society is ripe for political manipulation. "Human history becomes more and more a race between education and catastrophe," H. G. Wells once wrote. By focusing on entertainment rather than education, the news media increase the danger of our losing that race.

Throughout history, technology has had an impact on the nature of news, but not since the invention of the printing press half a millennium ago has it had as big an impact as today. New techno-splendours have miraculously expanded the opportunities for awareness of what is happening in the world through broadcasting, print, and the Internet. But these opportunities are too often being wasted and distorted in an avalanche of information. Two and a half millennia ago, Plato was worried about the same thing happening as a result of the invention of writing. In *Phaedrus*, Plato writes of Amon Ra, the sun god of the Egyptians, warning Thoth, the god of wisdom and magic, and scribe to the gods, who invented writing.

"You fool!" he says. "It is one thing to invent a thing, it's another to know the consequences. You think you have invented a remedy for the failure of memory, but what you have made is something that will make people lose it all. Having access to everything, they will think they know everything and they will become insufferable babblers."

"An information bomb is exploding in our midst, showering us with a shrapnel of images," says futurist Alvin Toffler in his book *The Third Wave*. Because of this "shrapnel," mass communication is giving way to boutique journalism and Plato's "insufferable babblers." The mass media are shrinking because the mass market is beginning to break up. Newspapers have been losing circulation (although the drop levelled off in 1997) and main networks have been losing audience in the last decade or so. In Europe, there were 3.5 million fewer daily papers sold each day in 1996 than in 1992, and in the United States the drop for the same period was 3 million. Canadian newspapers dropped in daily circulation from 5.8 million in 1990 to about 5 million in 1997. That drop likely will be arrested at least for a while, however, by the audacious arrival of Conrad Black's new national paper.

The same phenomenon is happening on television. In 1965, NBC, CBS, and ABC nightly newscasts were watched in 83 per cent of American homes, according to the Pew Research Center. *Time* says that by 1982 the figure was down to 41 per cent, and that in 1997 it was at an all-time low of 26.1 per cent. For prime-time programming in general, the drop is equally dramatic. In 1977, the main American networks had 92 per cent of the audience; twenty years later, they had 58 per cent. Canadian networks have similarly been losing viewers, with audiences dropping from a Nielsen fall rating estimate of 64 per cent in 1994 to 54 per cent in 1997. Specialty channel viewing in Canada has meanwhile been rising each year to a 1997 level of 27.4 per cent.

Alvin Toffler calls it a "demassified media." It is part of the overall trend towards individualism and single-issue politics. People feel more potent when they have more choice, but infinite choice also means anarchy in a socially fragmented society. As the new technology is used to package the news not so much for all of us collectively but more for each of us individually, there are fewer shared moments, thereby loosening national bonds and breeding instability. For democracy to work, there has to be a generally agreed upon set of facts and an identifying sense of community, but these are being eroded by the intense focus on the individual.

As a research tool, the Internet is a gold mine for reporters, and its chat groups, e-mail, and Web pages have made it the biggest self-publisher ever known, the ultimate vanity press. It is considered to be an instrument for empowering individuals because, in its early years, it has largely bypassed the gatekeeper – the journalist – in what's called "disintermediation." As a result, anyone with something to say can publish it on the Internet. But the quality of much of the information on the Internet is questionable because it is, indeed, a free-for-all. It is filled with amateur, would-be reporters unhindered by journalistic standards, experience, or accountability; by politicians and spin doctors selling a point of view; by experts whose credentials are suspect; and by charlatans, oddballs, and conspiracy addicts with hidden agendas and far-out theories.

There is danger, too, in news pouring onto the Internet or TV from untrained amateurs with home-video footage and on-the-scene reports. In Canada, there are probably about

2 million families with video cameras and in the United States, 30 to 40 million. As well, there are security cameras peering out in banks, airports, stores, hospitals, hotels, garages, freeways, apartment-building lobbies, and on street corners. They're everywhere. This new technology makes it easier, quicker, and cheaper to report on events with footage from non-traditional sources. There are significant advantages to this new wealth of visual news material in providing on-the-spot pictures of events not captured by professional cameras, such as the Rodney King beating by police in Los Angeles in 1991, captured on a home-video camera, or the Zapruder film of the assassination of President John F. Kennedy in Dallas. But while the spread of non-journalistic cameras provides valuable new sources of real news, it also releases a veritable flood of information about what's happening, with too little explanation of what it means. Analysis of events takes the brain power of thinking journalists, but increasingly they are being put out to pasture as being too expensive or too intellectually demanding.

The cacophony of voices on the Internet has made it an electronic tower of Babel, and quantity of information is being confused with quality of knowledge. Without the filter of journalistic expertise, much untrue, invalid information is passed off as real news. What journalists can provide as no others can is not only information, but explanation; they can point to cause and consequence. "To survive in the long run," says Neil Postman, "you must be in the meaning business." His comment underlines the importance of news organizations being on the Internet, doing what they can do best – gathering the news and putting it in context. It also underlines the importance of the mainstream media cleaning up their sensationalist practices.

The news media face profound change because of the new

technology, and since chaos is often an essential ingredient of change, we face a journalistically chaotic period for a decade or so. But if the media act as responsible, content-providing players in the cyberworld, they will retain their role as the glue of democracy. My long-term optimism about the future of journalism is rooted in the belief that the mainstream media will overcome their fascination with sensationalism and become responsible content providers not only in their newspapers and newscasts, but also on the Internet. I believe that public recognition and appreciation for the value of editorial navigators and brand-name quality journalism will make this happen. The Internet is, after all, essentially a means of delivery, a modern version of the old system of a kid selling papers on a street corner. The delivery system is secondary; the only thing that really matters is content.

"The lesson should be clear for everyone," CBC president Perrin Beatty says. "In a world of technological open borders, and technological fragmentation of the audience, you succeed on the merits of your content, or you don't succeed at all."

For the technologically sophisticated, the Internet is a mother lode of information, but as yet it does not dominate news distribution. Until it does, however – as it will – and until a more sober recognition of its social responsibility is adopted by the media, we are in danger of entering a dark age for journalism. Some media outlets offer quality reporting, but most do not. For the vast majority of people who still depend on print and broadcast news for their knowledge of what's happening, too much of what they are getting is being shaped by fear of the competition, by the quest for bigger profits, and by the misuse of technology. Most media emphasize shallow, bang-bang reportage designed to startle your eyeballs rather than engage your mind. In getting news without significance, context, and consequence, we run the danger of becoming a nation of voyeurs.

The Internet is the new competition for newspapers, but in recent years it has been fear of television that has driven much of the change in the print world, where magazines long ago gave up competing for general audiences. In the United States, *Saturday Evening Post*, *Life*, *Look*, and *Colliers* have all surrendered to specialized magazines such as *Money*, *Sports Illustrated*, *Gourmet Magazine*, and *Travel and Leisure*. Magazines are being forced to reinvent themselves as newspapers take on more of the style and complexion of newsmagazines. Given the changes in newspapers and competition from Internet news providers, it is likely that within the next decade, one of the three major newsmagazines in the United States – *Time*, *Newsweek*, and *U.S. News and World Report* – will go out of business. In Canada, *Maclean's* faces similar challenges, and will have to alter the nature of its content if it is to stay alive.

Most papers have fundamentally changed their presentation of the news, taking up a kind of talk-show culture. They have already given up trying to be first with the news, surrendering that role to broadcasting and now to the Internet. By chasing the passing whims of focus groups and surveys, most newspapers have shrivelled coverage of major political, economic, and social issues in favour of soft features, personality profiles, how-to advice, and a focus on the process rather than the substance of governance. Editors are spending less time considering content and much more on layout, graphics, typefaces, pictures, and grabby headlines.

Critics point to the phenomenon of the paparazzi chasing the rich and famous, with its sometimes tragic consequences, as with the death of Princess Diana, as a product of the media's thirst for sensationalism. Also to blame are the huge amounts of money the tabloid press is prepared to pay for inside tidbits and prying photos of celebrities. This is called "cash for trash." Since Princess Diana's death, there have been efforts to curb the paparazzi, but not necessarily for altruistic reasons. International media baron Rupert Murdoch – whose tabloids, including the *News of the World* and the *Sun* in Britain, are big buyers of the paparazzi's photographs – said within days of Diana's death that the pictures were all right, but "I'd say our newspapers paid far too much for them." But the paparazzi's manic quest for photos of Princess Diana and Emad Mohamed al-Fayed embracing, or similarly intrusive and intimate photos over the years of Grace Kelly, Marilyn Monroe, Elizabeth Taylor, and Jackie Kennedy Onassis, flow from the editorial values of the tabloids.

Federico Fellini's 1960 film *La Dolce Vita*, about postwar Roman decadence, featured Signore Paparazzo, a street photographer whose picture-taking persistence gave birth to the name paparazzi for his modern counterparts. The 1960s photographic technology used by Fellini's character, however, was far less intrusive than the powerful, automated digital cameras the paparazzi use today. The technology for invading privacy – cameras as small as buttons and recorders capable of picking up whispers in a street half a block away – has raced far ahead of ethics. The temptation to use such intrusive devices in search of hot gossip is irresistible to those whose idea of news is the latest scandal. Invasive photos are used to reinforce racy stories, such as the one in the *National Enquirer* a few days before her death, on the romance of Princess Diana and "Dodi" al-Fayed. It carried a front-page headline: "Di Goes Sex Mad: 'I Can't Get Enough.'"

One hundred and seventy-five years ago, U.S. President John Quincy Adams used to strip naked for a morning swim in the Potomac River in Washington, D.C., and nobody bothered him. Imagine the crowds of paparazzi if Bill Clinton tried that today!

The paparazzi phenomenon is part of the cult of personality, fostered and exploited by the tabloids, which increasingly pollutes the mainstream media. The public interest in this type of reportage is undeniable. In the week after Diana's death, British tabloid circulation rose sharply. Sales of the *News of the World* alone went up a quarter of a million copies. The tittle-tattle news, with its big headlines, intimate photos, short stories, and a fast-paced journalistic fizz, has been financially rewarding for certain newspaper proprietors. This approach, they know, is where the money is, and money is the object of their game. But a journalism that properly serves the public has to provide more than comic-book news and be driven by more than an obsession with profits; it has a responsibility to society as well as to stockholders. Canadian publisher Roy Thomson once said that news is "the stuff you separate the ads with," and he later told a Canadian royal commission, "My purpose is to run newspapers as a business . . . to make money." But journalism is more than a vehicle to deliver audiences to advertisers and profits to owners. "It is much more than a business," said the great *Manchester Guardian* editor C. P. Scott. "It reflects and influences the life of the whole community. . . . At the peril of its soul, it must see that the supply [of news] is not tainted."

Nowhere is that sentiment more germane than in television because, despite the efforts of newspapers to meet the challenge of television, most people now get their knowledge of what's happening from TV. And today TV is using dazzling new technology that is revolutionizing the way we see TV news and the way it is gathered and distributed. As happened when magazines became specialized, broadcasting is being replaced by narrowcasting. Thundering up behind, going a hundred miles an hour to God knows where, is the Internet with all its wonders and dangers, and behind the Internet comes the convergence of the TV screen and the computer monitor. Insofar as news delivery is concerned, the future isn't what it used to be; it's going infinitely faster and the changes are much more dramatic. Even the concept of national sovereignty is being altered as borders are made porous because of technological changes.

About a quarter of a century ago, as director of news and current affairs for the CBC, I found myself in front of three hundred high-school students at a national conference in Brandon, Manitoba, in a debate on the media with Canada's guru of communications technology, Marshall McLuhan. His exuberant rhetoric and complex jargon about the "global village" and the "medium is the message" frankly soared right over my earthbound head. I failed to understand let alone digest what he was talking about. But I think I've finally got his message and, like a roller coaster, it fills me with both chills and thrills.

I am far from being among the technological cognoscenti, but even a splash in the ocean of the Internet has been enough to make me realize something as fundamental as the invention of Gutenberg's press is happening out there in cyberspace. I agree with the American scientist Vannevar Bush, who once said, "We tend to overestimate the impact of technology in the short term and underestimate its impact in the long term." With the bandwidth potential of digital technology, you can forget about the five-hundred-channel universe that people have been talking about. Fox network officials are talking about a thousand channels by 2010, and, in time, there could be more like five thousand channels, with almost infinite specialization.

"The future of news is old hat," McLuhan once quipped, and while I'm not exactly sure what he meant, I've taken his words to be a comment on the speed of change in the electronic world, where yesterday's future is today's past. The advent of the Internet and the Web means that news is never going to be the same again. "It's the end of news . . . as we have known it," says Carleton University professor and author Roger Bird. Interactivity and hypertextuality are taking over.

In the United States and Canada, 60 million people (about 2 million in Canada) were on-line in early 1998, according to researchers. The figures are soaring, and while there likely will be a lingering role for some paper and ink newspapers and abbreviated network TV newscasts, within a couple of decades, we may well get most of our news from the Internet, viewed on a converged TV and computer screen.

"The Internet is a global mind because it's active," says Derrick de Kerckhove, the director of the University of Toronto's McLuhan Program in Culture and Technology. "TV is a global village because it's passive." If true, this surely means that in the future TV will focus on entertainment for passive couch potatoes, while the Internet will be the source of challenging, active, and interactive information. As a consequence, de Kerckhove believes, the active citizen will be much better informed because of the Internet. But that depends, of course, on the quality of the content on the Internet.

Traditional ways of delivering the news are indeed becoming, as McLuhan suggested, "old hat." "Eventually all information will be conveyed on your television computer," says Carnegie Mellon University research scientist Dr. Robert H. Thibadeau. Most successful newspaper, radio, and television operators may well be largely out of the business of delivering the news in a couple of decades or so. They may no longer be in the "pipeline" business, so to speak, but rather in the product business. To rephrase a popular political slogan: "It's the content, stupid!" How the product gets delivered to the public is less important than the product itself. Journalism is software, not hardware. Unless this is understood, newspapers will be driven into bankruptcy and broadcasters into banality. In a world with thousands of communications satellites whirling around the globe, sending and receiving signals from cameras and computers, the Internet will be our principal news-distribution system, not paper, ink, presses, and delivery trucks, and not network television as we know it today.

The new technology encourages live or near-live TV coverage of events, and this has given rise to ethical problems. "The amount of time between when footage is shot and when it is aired has decreased significantly," says the Radio–Television News Directors Association (RTNDA), which represents broadcast newsrooms in Canada and the United States, "thus eliminating a buffer zone during which reporters and editors can consider the ethical ramifications of broadcasting the information. Many respondents [to an RTNDA survey] also worry that the line between news programs and 'tabloid' or 'sensational' journalism will grow more blurry."

"Organizations are squeezing their journalists to perform faster and faster and doing more and more of the work with less and less human support," says Canadian media expert Pauline Couture. "As a result . . . very young people with boundless energy and nerves steeled in part by ignorance of the consequences make momentous decisions on our behalf. . . . Young reporters working alone under exhausting circumstances can do a lot of damage. . . . It's easy to look upon these technologies as a life line out of the pressure created by budget cuts, but they are not a panacea. The technologies are a tool. And as with any other tool, the most important thing is what you're going to do with it."

Some broadcasters have been testing newscasts tailored to individual interests. Some futurists go much further, foreseeing individually tailored news delivered to a magazine-sized, portable screen. This designer edition would be an inkless, paperless, pressless, and truckless electronic newspaper on a computer that could be carried in a briefcase. It would not only keep one in touch with the latest news anywhere in the world at any time, but would be a one-stop business and personal communicator. The Knight-Ridder newspaper chain in the United States, among others, is already working on such an instrument.

But unless we are incurably addicted to speed and quantity, ink, paper, and presses won't totally and immediately disappear because, while computers or TV screens can pour out data, they cannot yet provide the quietly absorbing environment needed for serious reading and thinking. A book, Derrick de Kerckhove says, is "a resting place for words." So, too, is a serious newspaper as, he adds, "Television may give you the experience, but the newspaper gives you the meaning." The newspapers, magazines, and books that survive in paper form for at least a few decades into the twenty-first century will be those providing the meaning of information.

Amid this whirlwind of change, most of the media are thrashing about with splashy layouts, pop news, colour, and focus groups to find out what audiences and readers want. New technology is being used not so much to enrich the news, but to make it more popular. One example of this comes from not-so-new technology: helicopters. To amortize the expense of the equipment, broadcasters are using helicopters for much more than rush-hour traffic reports. University of Southern California professor and media expert Jeffrey Cole surveyed Los Angeles TV stations and found helicopters being used for coverage of car chases, brush fires, bank robberies, parades, protest marches, riots and rallies, as well as traffic reports. As many as eight or nine TV helicopters circle some events. A vivid example of this was the helicopter chase of suspected murderer O. J. Simpson down a Los Angeles freeway, which was broadcast live for hours to an audience of nearly 100 million. The visual drama of helicopter coverage has resulted, Cole found, in a sharp increase in such news on the air and, since newscast time is finite, a consequent decrease in reporting on political, social, and economic issues and events. One Los Angeles helicopter news pilot, Lawrence Welk III, whose musical grandfather was a TV star, says, "I am in the entertainment business. . . . I bring them action and tragedy."

A classic example of that "action and tragedy" was the live helicopter coverage of a suicide on a Los Angeles freeway in the spring of 1998. A distraught man got out of his pickup truck, unfurled a banner protesting inadequate health care, and, after an hour of tying up traffic and defying police, set himself on fire. A few minutes later he shoved a shotgun under his chin and pulled the trigger. All of it was seen live on television, thanks to the hovering news helicopters of several Los Angeles TV stations. Two of the stations interrupted children's programs to provide the live suicide coverage, which was also carried nationally by the cable channel MSNBC.

Half a dozen years ago, TV news carried another on-camera suicide when, at a televised news conference, the treasurer of Pennsylvania pulled out a gun and killed himself. Some stations later showed the suicide in full, some stopped short just before he fired the gun and fell. These incidents provide a haunting echo of Paddy Chayefsky's film *Network*, which portrayed a live, on-camera suicide designed to boost ratings.

All these technological marvels, from helicopters to interactive Web sites, combined with the broadcasters' profit imperative and a perception that audience attention spans are getting ever shorter, are having a profound impact on broadcast news. At the same time, Canadian radio and TV stations are sharply cutting back on newsroom staff. With a few exceptions such as the CBC, Canadian radio has already abandoned serious journalism, substituting endless varieties of music, brief headlines, and opinionated loudmouths on cheap-to-produce call-in shows.

American "Shock Jock" Howard Stern is a vivid example of this. When he arrived on the air in Montreal and Toronto in late 1997, he caused a sharp increase in ratings for the stations carrying his insults and manipulation of issues and events. "The biggest scumbags on the planet, as I've said all along, are not only the French in France, but the French in Canada," Stern declared on air. "Anybody who speaks French is a scumbag. It turns you into a coward. . . . The French were the first ones to cave in to the Nazis."

Stern's objective is to entertain by shock, not to enlighten. Preoccupied with entertaining and not informing listeners, like most of his radio colleagues across the country, Toronto's Q107 program director Pat Cardinal told the *Globe and Mail*, "It's extremely gratifying. Howard Stern has had an outstanding effect." Stern's fulminations pushed CHOM-FM into the number-one position in the Montreal English market in its first ratings period, although the ratings slipped later on. "The introduction of Howard Stern has simply been the biggest story in the history of Canadian radio," said CHOM-FM general manager Lee Hambleton, looking at ratings that gave Stern more than 1.1 million Canadian listeners weekly.

In television, executives are terrified of the remote-control channel changer in the hands of what they see as easily bored TV nomads, zapping their way across the dial. It used to be that you had to get up and walk over to the TV set to change channels, but when remote-control channel changers came along, viewers were freed from the dictates of programmers. Ever since, producers have sought ways to keep viewers' fingers off the zapper. They believe that most people invest about fifteen seconds on serious issues before they change the channel. Consequently, they are convinced that those who will dominate news and current-affairs programming in the twenty-first century will be those who can keep their audience for longer than fifteen seconds. This has brought the likes of Geraldo Rivera and other camp followers who seek to entertain and shock in the guise of reflecting social issues. While most are American programs, they're seen widely in Canada, too, including the show hosted by Jerry Springer, the king of trash TV, which reaches about 10 million Americans and Canadians every weekday (300,000 in southern Ontario) – making it one of the most watched daytime talk shows in North America. Topics include "I'm Pregnant by a Transsexual," "Women with Watermelon Breasts," "I Have Sex with My Sister," "My Sister Slept with My Three Husbands."

As a result of the preoccupation with fast-paced trivia, TV networks and stations are cutting back significantly on serious news, especially political coverage. Reporting on the 1996 U.S. presidential election campaign on NBC, CBS, and ABC was down 55 per cent compared to 1992 coverage, according to the Annenberg Public Policy Center in Washington, D.C. It looks likely that the networks' coverage will fall even further in the year 2000, the next election year, as they leave reporting on the details of the campaign to specialized channels and the Internet.

Surveys also show the average sound bite in the campaign coverage of presidential candidates on U.S. network main newscasts has dropped from about forty-two seconds thirty years ago to about eight seconds in the 1996 election. Eight seconds is far from adequate time to set out a political position and so, in response, astute politicians have learned the art of simplistic sloganeering. This trend in coverage is almost as true in Canada as it is in the United States, even though an Angus Reid poll in the spring of 1998 showed only 20 per cent of Canadians wanted to see less coverage of politics and government.

Television's response to the perceived short attention span of the viewer too often is to provide a P. T. Barnum offering of racy stories, soft, cuddly features, and bloody crime. "Headless Body in Topless Bar" (a front-page headline published by Rupert Murdoch's *New York Post*) is the ideal headline for the "If it bleeds it leads" school of journalism. Increasingly, accidents, fires, murders, sexual oddities, natural disasters, personality news, how-to features, and pee-wee reports of political conflict make up the news, especially on local stations. Canadian stations, according to a study by the Fraser Institute in Vancouver, focus on what it calls "chaos" news – crime, accidents, and natural disasters – at about half the rate of American stations. "Chaos" coverage on Canadian stations accounts for 22 per cent of local news while for U.S. stations the figure is 40 per cent, reports the Fraser Institute.

In mid-1997, a study by eight U.S. universities showed that American local TV stations were devoting an average of 30 per cent of their newscasts to crime stories – twice as much time as given to coverage of government and politics. Race-relations coverage received 1.2 per cent of airtime. A late-1997 study by the Center for Media and Public Affairs in Washington, D.C., showed that crime was the favourite topic for the main newscasts on NBC, CBS, and ABC. The number of crime stories carried by the three networks in 1993–96 was three times that of the early 1990s, with murder stories up by more than 700 per cent. In the same period, the U.S. crime rate fell by 20 per cent to its lowest level in thirty years. The same survey showed that there were more network newscast stories devoted to the O. J. Simpson murder case than to events in the Middle East.

The media's glamorization and exploitation of American crime has seeped north across the border. Crime is easier and cheaper to cover than politics and economics, and while Canadian newscasts are not so dominated by crime stories as U.S. news programs, Canadian stations nevertheless are being lured into expanding coverage of deviant behaviour. In addition, some cable packages that supply U.S. programs to areas of Western Canada have used Detroit stations as the source of their American programming, and crime is a big item on the newscasts of those stations. Even though the Detroit murders, assaults, and robberies they see on TV happened fifteen hundred miles away, many Prairie residents have shaped some of their political attitudes on the basis of what they have seen of crime in the motor city. According to an Angus Reid survey, most Canadians today, especially those in Western Canada, are alarmed about increasing crime in their communities, even though official studies show a significant and steady drop in most crime across the country in recent years. The survey said 59 per cent of Canadians believe the crime rate is rising, while only 8 per cent of Canadians believe the official statistics about the falling rates.

Crime reporting is the key reason for this growing Canadian apprehension, says Angus Reid senior vice-president John Wright. "People are sensitized to it because it makes news, because it's in their face every day." In general, violence on TV outruns violence in society, and, with the disproportionate emphasis on crime in many newscasts and newspapers, it's no wonder that there are constant demands for political actions to cure the problem even though it's not there to the extent most people believe. And when the news and discussion of government and politics is squeezed by news of crime and trivialities, the dialogue of democracy is threatened.

If we continue our descent into triviality, most news stories will be shorter, simpler, less researched, and will run the risk of error and distortion by brevity. This is especially true for coverage of international events. Foreign news bureaus for broadcasters and newspapers are closing around the world in cost-cutting frenzies. Coverage in the case of most newspapers has been left to freelancers or to news agencies, which themselves have been cutting back on staff. "One hundred years from now, historians looking back at the papers and news programs will scratch their heads wondering what was going on," says the CBC's veteran correspondent David Halton. For Canadian newspapers, most of the foreign news we read comes from a foreign perspective, written by American reporters with the Associated Press or, to a smaller extent, by British reporters working for Reuters. This inevitably means that the foreign news bears American or British references, and reflects their assumptions and values.

In TV's case, foreign correspondents are being replaced by young enthusiasts, journalistically inexperienced but aggressively peripatetic, who gallop around the globe with new lightweight cameras in search of dramatic pictures that will excite if not enlighten. Explanation, background, and nuances are out; immediacy, drama, and conflict are in. Aggravating the lack of depth is the ever-diminishing time between action and reaction. Live reportage of events serves the purpose of drama but limits thinking time for journalists.

I vividly recall how in the late 1960s the absence of modern technology compelled me to do more textured coverage on the Vietnam War than just reporting on what we called "the bang-bang." The American networks fed their news out of Saigon daily by satellite, providing a sense of immediacy by showing Vietnam fire fights that had just happened. They believed immediacy was reality. But the CBC couldn't afford daily satellite feeds, and if I or my colleagues covered the battles, our reports would have been badly outdated by the time they were flown back to Canada. For example, near the so-called demilitarized zone dividing North and South Vietnam, I once tramped through the jungle with a U.S. Marine unit, reporting on their mission. I handed the film to a jeep driver, who took it to a nearby helicopter base. From there it was flown to Da Nang, then put on another plane to Saigon, where it was put on yet another plane to Hong Kong. It was then flown to Vancouver and finally on to Toronto, where four or five days after it was filmed, the report got on the air.

Because of the time I knew my report would take to get to Toronto, I was forced to focus on the significance and background of what was happening, not just the bang bang in front of me. In short, I had a buffer zone for thought that was denied those reporters who had more immediate deadlines in getting on the satellite feeds to New York. Ironically, as a result of the CBC not being able to afford satellite technology, I think Canadians were better informed and had a broader perspective than Americans about the root causes, implications, and background of the war in Vietnam.

While the U.S. networks did provide thoughtful coverage from time to time, their emphasis was on the immediate reporting of events because they had the technology to do so. There was simply more blood in a satellite news story than in a story done on film. "New York wants John Wayne movies," one U.S. network correspondent in Vietnam told me. It was much the same story years later in the Gulf War, where, going Vietnam one better, technology allowed and news directors encouraged live coverage of air raids and battle scenes. But, as so often happens, the immediate coverage crowded out reflective reports on events.

David Halton, now the CBC correspondent in Washington, encountered the same situation on his posting to Paris in 1966. "Because we couldn't afford to do daily satellite feeds and had to ship film by air," Halton says, "we would do less crisis coverage and more interpretive and analytical reporting, pieces that would be more thoughtful and would be as valuable tomorrow as today. In a way, satellites and other technology increased a tendency to encourage fire-engine coverage. In many ways, as technology improved, the quality of reporting declined."

A nodding head of agreement comes from the former CBCer Robert MacNeil, who became one of the most distinguished journalists in U.S. television with the *MacNeil/Lehrer Report* on PBS. Forecasting the end of television news as we know it, MacNeil says, "I am pessimistic because all the trends in television journalism are towards the sensational, the hype, the hyperactive, the tabloid values that drive out the serious."

Not only is quality down, but so, too, is quantity. U.S. network coverage of foreign affairs in their main newscasts has been cut by about half in the last decade, and there have been similar reductions of foreign coverage in U.S. and Canadian newspapers. The Canadian media, however, have always carried more international news than their American counterparts, and never more so than now with the Cold War over and no "evil empire" to kick around any more. U.S. coverage of foreign news is, at best, a lick and a promise because editors and producers in the New York newsrooms believe the public simply isn't interested in what's going on in other countries. Most foreign coverage has been reduced to news of wars, famines, and top-level diplomacy. The foreign stories that are carried are about half the length or less than they were a decade ago. The three- or four-minute report has given way to ninety-second reports. As a result, networks find it harder to justify the expense of foreign correspondents.

The nature of foreign news has changed, too, because of technology. In the 1950s and 1960s, knowledgeable correspondents were based in capitals around the world, soaking up background on the area and providing well-textured reports of what was happening, why, and what it meant. But then jet planes came on the scene, enabling reporters to get from New York, London, or Toronto to a news hot spot in half the time it used to take. Network and newspaper managers quickly realized that foreign coverage would cost far less if they had "firemen" reporters flying out from network headquarters to chase "bang-bang" stories. This approach meant foreign-base housing and living allowances could be eliminated, as could the cost of foreign offices, cars, and technical support. Besides, they reasoned, the "firemen" reporters, leaping from story to story around the globe, would cover more stories and give the networks and newspapers more usage of them. The one factor the managers ignored, though, was that however much the firemen reporters boned up on the jet en route to the story, they could never match the local knowledge of a foreign-based correspondent.

When satellites came along, the networks began dismantling even more foreign bureaus, claiming they could do as good a job or better with the "firemen." It's not true, of course, and the result is the public gets less and poorer quality foreign news. One reason for the paucity of international news reporting in the United States, says renowned *Washington Post* owner Katharine Graham, is that it "will not bring in a single page of advertising." In his 1996 book *International News and Foreign Correspondents*, Stephen Hess argues that because foreign news offered to Americans today is sharply deficient, Americans are increasingly ill-informed about what's going on in the world. Shrinking foreign news coverage not only is occurring in the United States and Canada, but in most other media-rich nations, too, for reasons of cost and perceived lack of interest.

While international reportage in mainstream newscasts has fallen off, the distribution of news by satellite to countries on every continent has sharply increased. CNN began it, and today satellites are pumping out the news to nations around the world, not only from CNN, but from Rupert Murdoch's Star and Sky Services, NBC, BBC, a host of European services, and, on a much smaller scale, the CBC's Newsworld International.

Except for CNN, none of them is making much, if any, money, but the competition is nevertheless fierce and the drive to find new markets for satellite news can sometimes conflict with journalistic ethics and honesty. Some countries view the beamed-in news as politically or culturally offensive, if not subversive. Faced with the loss of sales or the loss of integrity, the satellite news deliverers' answer too often favours sales over integrity. When China complained about the BBC's news coverage carried by Rupert Murdoch's Star system, Murdoch dropped the BBC. China also complained when NBC sports reporter Bob Costas mentioned human-rights problems in China as the Chinese athletes came into the Atlanta stadium during the 1996 Summer Olympics. NBC, owned by General Electric, which has large commercial interests in China, quickly apologized, saying, "The comments were not based on NBC beliefs."

China's sensitivity to international satellite news can be traced to television journalists' sympathetic coverage of the nascent democracy movement in China when it was brutally suppressed in Tiananmen Square. China's sensitivity extends to the free flow of information on the Internet. In 1998, it imposed severe restrictions on any Internet information that, in Beijing's judgement, endangered "social security."

Outright fakery in the news is another problem that is showing up more often than it used to, even back in the 1930s and 1940s in the old March of Time newsreels, which frequently used undeclared re-enactments. For instance, Italian freelancers sold to the American networks "footage" of the 1986 Chernobyl nuclear explosion. After it was aired, the networks found out it was, in reality, footage of a smoky factory in Italy's Po Valley. CBS was taken in by a freelancer who walked into the London bureau with a vivid atrocity tape from Bosnia, showing Muslims slaughtering a Serb village. It was, however, faked, as CBS later learned. In the Afghanistan War, correspondents were deluged with offers of dramatic tape of battles, but none of it was verifiable.

Sometimes faked footage goes on air because budget-cutting has forced a reliance on freelancers, many of whom are more interested in selling their product than meeting journalistic standards. But sometimes, too, the fraud is perpetrated by reporters untrained in journalistic ethics. This happened when NBC's 1992 *Dateline* program faked a truck explosion to dramatize the producer's belief that the vehicle was unsafe; and when Janet Cooke of the *Washington Post* faked a report on an eight-year-old heroin addict, a story that won her a Pulitzer Prize before her deceit was uncovered. And there are times when plain old stupidity, not cupidity, is the cause of misinformation. Short-cut investigative journalism is, however, a disservice to the public and to the current patron saints of investigative journalism, reporters Bob Woodward and Carl Bernstein of the *Washington Post*, whose dogged, detailed fact-checking about the break-in at Watergate triggered the downfall of President Richard Nixon.

Media credibility may get much shakier with the use of new digital wonders. Since our technology is running ahead of our ethics, it becomes ever more tempting to slice, dice, and re-arrange video or still pictures easily and undetectably. The fictional Forrest Gump was seen standing beside Kennedy,

Johnson, and Nixon; in the real world, people can also be seen to be with others they have never met or in places they have never been, and background figures can be eliminated or added, or any rearrangement made.

Anyone and anything can be morphed into something it isn't. As ads for the 1998 movie comedy *Wag the Dog* proclaimed, "A Hollywood producer, a Washington spin doctor. When they get together, they can make you believe anything." In Britain, photos in the *News of the World* of a holidaying Princess Diana and "Dodi" al-Fayed, shown just before their deaths, were digitally "enhanced" to show them about to kiss. *Time* magazine altered reality in a cover photo of O. J. Simpson by making his face darker and more menacing than it was in the original photograph. The *National Geographic* magazine once moved the pyramids a touch closer together in a photo to make a more dramatic shot. In 1997, *Newsweek* magazine digitally doctored a cover photo of a mother of newborn septuplets to make her teeth whiter and straighter than they were in the original photo. In fact, numerous national magazines in Canada and the United States "enhance" photos to eliminate wrinkles, moles, and scars. But an altered photo or tape, even for cosmetic purposes, is a lie and, used on the news, it undermines media credibility.

The new technology concept of "virtual reality" presents other problems. While it holds enormous potential for medicine, science, education, and other areas, it holds dangers for journalism because although the image may be virtually the same as the real thing, it isn't exactly the same. A reporter standing in an office can be seen to be in a war zone, a newsroom, a parade, or anywhere, and the audience can't tell the difference. This happened in the mid-1990s when an ABC producer had a Washington correspondent put on her coat and deliver a report standing in her office. The background was faked, however, and she appeared to be standing outside the U.S. Capitol building.

What happens in a world where reality is sometimes virtual, but not real? The danger, I believe, is that when reality is "improved" and the trivial predominates, people are, in effect, being subjected to political, social, and economic manipulation. They have less ability to evaluate the implications of what's happening and become misinformed and cynical.

The so-called news "spinners" or "opinion engineers" in Ottawa, Washington, and other centres of political power believe perception *is* reality. They want the biases and the perceptions of their political or corporate bosses to dominate the news, not somebody else's. As a result, political debate is degraded. Rant prevails over reason when sloganeering charlatans con the public with emotion and brevity, making people certain about things of which they know little.

Deceitful use of the new technology in the news may well cause the fissure between aware and unaware citizens to grow to a chasm, as the affluent, smart, and technologically adept effectively mine the information-rich cyberworld, while the poor and technologically inept are entertained but not enlightened.

About thirty-five years ago, the historian and social critic Daniel Boorstin gloomily foresaw a landscape of couch potatoes living, he said, "in a world where fantasy is more real than reality, where image has more dignity than its original." Even Pope John Paul II has lamented what he called the "evil" intentions of some of the media. "Public opinion has been shocked," he said, "at how easily the advanced communications technologies can be exploited by those whose intentions are evil. . . . The truth of the matter may well be that the foremost value they generally represent is commercial profit."

An answer to the concerns of the Pope, Boorstin, and others was provided by long-time University of Chicago head Robert Maynard Hutchins, who offered a seminal study on news in 1947. In it, he proposed five central functions for the media:

1. Provide a "truthful, comprehensive account of the day's events in a context that gives them meaning."
2. Provide a "forum for the exchange of comment and criticism."
3. Provide a "representational picture of the constituent groups of society."
4. Provide and clarify the "goals and values of society."
5. Provide "full access to the day's intelligence."

In the fifty years since the Hutchins report, the quantity of news has expanded phenomenally and a handful of news organizations have reached out for the objectives it set, including the *Daily Telegraph*, the *Economist*, the *New York Times*, the *Globe and Mail*, and the BBC and the CBC. Most of the media, however, haven't come close as they skim from event to event with, at best, a passing glance at the principles Hutchins recommended.

In the last sixty years, much of the media seem to have gone through three broad phases: lapdog journalism in the period from the Second World War to the assassination of John F. Kennedy; watchdog journalism from Vietnam to Watergate; and junkyard journalism since then, epitomized by the coverage of the O. J. Simpson murder case and of the sexploits of the Royals and the American presidents.

New technology has been used to amplify the interesting, the sensational, the odd, the conflicting, and the controversial. But, with few exceptions, it has not been used nearly so much to illustrate social issues, political substance, and economic debate. This has left the immediate triumphant over the reflective, the surface over the substance. Although he was speaking of an older medium, George Bernard Shaw's comment strikes a contemporary bell: "Newspapers are unable seemingly to discriminate between a bicycle accident and the collapse of civilization." More vividly, former British prime minister Stanley Baldwin said in the 1920s that too many journalists enjoy "power without responsibility; the power of the harlot throughout the ages."

As that kid on the corner hustling newspapers nearly six decades ago, I was trying to entertain more than to enlighten. It took me a few more years before I recognized that journalists are, or should be, teachers, not entertainers.

2

Empty Heads
and Pinheads

"**A** people without reliable news is sooner or later a people without the basis of freedom," British political scientist Harold Laski once said. "The health of society depends upon the quality of the information it receives" was columnist Walter Lippmann's view. Their comments underscore the reality that in an increasingly complex, interrelated, speed-obsessed world, the nature of news is critical and the reliability of news is essential.

An independent, responsible media are a prerequisite for democracy as an invaluable monitor of government and society. In a democracy, we stake everything on the rational dialogue of an informed public, and journalism is the central instrument of that dialogue. A nation of empty heads will produce a government of pinheads because a real, participatory democracy simply can't survive without a professional and socially responsible media providing the raw material for public debate and public opinion.

Without comprehensive, thorough, fair reportage on the events and issues of the day, the public is forced to make judge-

ments and cast votes based on gossip, rumours, and speculation. As the quality of public knowledge of current developments sinks with a down-market media, the quality of
government also sinks, and the temptation for autocracy rises.

The media's responsibility is to reflect reality, even when
that requires noting that some powers-that-be are economiz-
ing on truth. Media loyalty lies first with the public; they are, in
effect, agents for the public.

At the end of the twentieth century, issues and events are
moving so quickly and becoming so complicated and interrelated that there seem to be no clear solutions to anything
any more, just trade-offs. The media's role is to indicate what's
being traded off for what gains and what losses.

While there are numerous power centres in any democracy
– elected representatives, government mandarins, the judi-
ciary, the business community, labour unions – it is the media
that essentially bind it all together because they provide the
forum for the presentation and discussion of information and
ideas. The media reflect a nation talking to itself, informing,
explaining, analysing, looking to the future, reporting various
political, social, and economic viewpoints, and showing social
cooperation as well as social confrontation. Without journalism, there would be a universal sense of uncertainty, because
the public simply wouldn't know what was going on. As Graham
Spry, the father of public broadcasting in Canada, said, "Information is the prime, integrating factor in creating, nourishing,
adjusting, and sustaining a society."

Journalism, I believe, is the hinge of democracy, the critical link between the governed and the governing. It may be
hasty, incomplete, and frequently flawed, but it is an imperfect necessity for a functioning democracy. The effectiveness

of a socially responsible media directly influences the effectiveness of our democracy.

In many ways, it was the Second World War that elevated journalism to being a respected profession. People depended on the media to tell them of the great battles, of Allied strategy, of the giants of the time – Sir Winston Churchill, Franklin Delano Roosevelt, and Joseph Stalin – and of what their far-away sons were doing. After the war, coverage of international events expanded far beyond anything done before, and schools of journalism blossomed at universities across the land. The dream of most young would-be journalists, as was mine at the time, was to be a foreign correspondent or a Parliament Hill reporter, writing about the great issues of the day.

News had become a thoughtful business, and most front pages of Canadian dailies reflected that with detailed stories from Ottawa, Washington, London, Paris, or Moscow. Sensationalism had flourished in the 1930s partly as an antidote to the miseries of the Depression. Traces of journalistic extravagance remained in some papers in the 1940s and '50s, but it was the exception, not the rule.

Throughout the postwar and Cold War years, the central focus of most news organizations was on serious journalism for serious times. When the Iron Curtain came crashing down in 1989, however, suddenly there was no more of the news-generating East–West confrontation. Foreign news coverage began to slip as newspapers, radio, and TV searched for ways to replace the Cold War news stories. At the same time, reading, listening, and watching the news began falling off.

Without the commanding tensions of the Cold War to cover, little by little the news media began sliding towards softer news and feature reports, and, in recent years, seeking popularity by starting to ape the supermarket tabloids. As competition intensified with the arrival of CNN, Newsworld, and other specialized TV channels, and then the Internet, long-held standards began wavering. If news had been too professorial in the 1950s and '60s, by the late 1990s it had become too much like the barker at an old-time carnival show.

The media, in all their forms, have been central to the governing of nations from the days of the *Roman Gazette*, through the news criers and newsletters of the Middle Ages, to the radio and television of today, and, increasingly, to the Internet. In the early days of print, Sir Francis Bacon remarked that printed newsletters changed "the state of the whole world."

Since the beginning of the profession, there have been three basic types of journalism: authoritarian, libertarian, and socially responsible. Authoritarian journalism prevailed until well into the 1700s, providing news that supported the rulers. Libertarian journalism, which flourished in the 1800s, gave readers point-of-view news, with no attempt at balance, and an abundance of biased reporting. It was left to the news consumer to seek out the truth from comparing many reports. Socially responsible reportage, a relatively new concept, seeks a fair reflection of the facts untarnished by bias and clearly separated from point-of-view commentaries.

With the shift of power from the upper classes to the masses in much of the world beginning around the turn of the twentieth century, it became critical in making democracy work to be certain the masses had reliable, substantive information on what was happening and what it meant. Junk news was not enough. More than half a century ago, journalist Walter Lippmann wrote of the expanding responsibility of journalism, saying, "The power to determine each day what shall be seen important and what shall be neglected is a power unlike any that has been exercised since the Pope lost his hold on the secular mind." Telling it "the way it is," as Walter Cronkite used to say as he ended his newscasts, gave journalism a power it had not previously enjoyed. "Free public discussion of public affairs, notwithstanding its incidental mischief, is the breath of life for parliamentary institutions," said Sir Lyman Duff, Canada's chief justice from 1933 to 1944.

What the public read in the papers was pivotal in bringing about the American Revolution and critical in bringing political reforms to Canada as we edged away from colonialism, and what people saw on television was crucial in ending the Vietnam War and decisive in the collapse of the Iron Curtain. "I fear three newspapers more than a thousand bayonets," Napoleon once said, and well he might. Some years after the right to report parliamentary debate freely was established in England in the late 1700s, Thomas Carlyle understood what it meant. He looked up at the press gallery in parliament and noted, "In the Reporters' Gallery yonder [sits] a fourth estate, more important far than them all."

When the United States began its life, Thomas Jefferson went even further, saying, "Were it left to me to decide whether we should have a government without newspapers, or newspapers without a government, I should not hesitate a moment to prefer the latter."

Dictators, tyrants, and autocrats through the ages have sought to control the media, but in the end, technology in one form or another has defeated them. "Why should a government which is doing what it believes to be right, allow itself to be criticized?" asked Vladimir Lenin in 1920. "Why should any man be allowed to buy a printing press and disseminate pernicious opinions calculated to embarrass the government?" It was a good question, and the answer came seventy years later when Western television and radio signals and Internet communications leapt over the Iron Curtain with their democratic messages. That was the end of Lenin's communism. Roman emperors asked the same question, as did the Tudor kings of England and twentieth-century dictators. Autocrats may be able to suppress local news, but technology bearing messages of freedom has hurdled over their barriers.

Today, when nothing is standing still and variables outnumber the constants, technology has presented us with what may yet prove to be the ultimate shaper of public opinion – the Internet. Through cyberspace, we now have what the 1971 Davey Report on Mass Media scoffingly dismissed as "a land of bubblegum forests and lollipop trees [where] every man would have his own newspaper or a broadcasting station devoted exclusively to programming that man's opinions and perceptions."

In principle, the idea of everybody publishing his own view and reading or hearing or seeing everything in the news from every political viewpoint is the libertarian approach to news that John Milton advocated in the 1600s when he argued for a free marketplace of ideas. Milton was echoed three centuries later by American Supreme Court Justice Hugo Black when he said, "The widest possible dissemination of information from diverse and antagonistic sources is essential to the welfare of the public. [It is] a condition of a free society." In practice, however, in today's advanced technological environment, it is hopelessly impractical for people to read, hear, and see everything. We are simply swamped with bits and pieces of information. Technology makes so much available to us so fast that there isn't enough time to absorb "all the news that's fit to print," as the *New York Times* boasts, or fit to broadcast, let alone all the news from all the viewpoints. More than ever before we need knowledgeable and trusted editorial guides to lead us through the avalanche of news. "History is just one damn thing after another," Winston Churchill once said, and that applies to journalism as well, for journalism is history in the present tense, tumbling, jumbling all around us.

One of those "damn things" to which Churchill referred is the overwhelming impact the media have on our political processes. Prime ministers, presidents, all political leaders view managing the media as a vital precondition to their managing the legislature, the public, and the whole political process. "Where there is a free press, the governors must live in constant awe of the opinions of the governed," said English historian and author Thomas Babington Macaulay. Political campaigns are dominated by each party's need to get its message in the papers and, even more important, on TV.

Mackenzie King was staggered by the new technology of radio when, on July 1, 1927, he spoke to the nation in a live broadcast from Parliament Hill on our sixtieth anniversary as a country. "All of Canada became a single assemblage," he marvelled in his diary. ". . . [I]t is doubtful if ever before . . . those in authority were brought into such immediate and sympathetic personal touch with those from whom their authority derived." There was "nothing comparable," he said, realizing radio would change politics forever, just as the printing press had done a few centuries earlier and television would do three decades later.

In the United States a few years later, Franklin Delano Roosevelt also discovered the political value of radio with his Fireside Chats, which allowed him to talk directly to the public. Richard Nixon was both saved and killed by television:

saved by the sympathetic way he came across with his corny "Checkers speech," when he pleaded not to be thrown off the 1952 Eisenhower presidential ticket, and later killed by what the nation saw of him during the Watergate scandal. Television smiled on John F. Kennedy, giving him a presidential election momentum he never relinquished after his first televised campaign debate with Nixon. Ronald Reagan was so popular as a president because he was made for TV. With his actor's training, gee-whiz smile, and friendly demeanour, he effectively demonstrated the political virtue of appearance over substance. In so much of contemporary political life, sadly, pleasing images and sound-bite comments seem to be what matter.

Recognizing the power of TV, Prime Minister Lester Pearson at one point barred his cabinet ministers from appearing on the CBC program *This Hour Has Seven Days* lest they be led into making a politically ruinous comment. Czech President Vaclav Havel was taken aback at how important television was to him. "I never fail to be astonished at how much I am at the mercy of television directors and editors, at how my public image depends far more on them than it does on myself," he said.

When President Lyndon Johnson saw Walter Cronkite tell his CBS television audience that the United States could not win the war in Vietnam, he remarked to an aide, "If we've lost Cronkite, we've lost the war." Later, although the *Washington Post* had spearheaded the exposé of the Watergate cover-up, it wasn't until Cronkite aired two major reports on the scandal that it seized the nation's attention. No wonder the polls showed that Cronkite had become, through television, "the most trusted man in America."

To me, as a correspondent covering the American civil-rights clashes and walking the streets of Selma, Alabama, following

Dr. Martin Luther King, Jr. or nervously walking through the riot-torn areas of Newark, Detroit, and Los Angeles, the power of the media was amply evident. Protesters suddenly came alive with noise when the TV cameras pointed their way. Indeed, the footage of Sheriff Bull Connor letting loose his German shepherds on demonstrators in Birmingham, Alabama, did more for the cause of civil rights than anything else. "I have a dream . . ." said Martin Luther King a few months later at a Washington demonstration. It made for a powerful TV and newspaper image and it was a critical persuader in the public debate over civil rights in the United States.

Television news has become an extension of politics and diplomacy. Presidents and prime ministers can hear faster about what's going on from CNN, the BBC World Service, and the CBC's Newsworld than from their own officials and ambassadors. Television, as it did in the Gulf War, can take viewers live to the battlefield to watch a bombing raid as it is happening. Political leaders use radio and TV to send messages around the globe to friend and foe alike. When Nikita Khrushchev blinked and put an end to the Cuban Missile Crisis, he did it on Moscow Radio. When George Bush warned Saddam Hussein, he did it on television. When Boris Yeltsin defied a military take-over in Moscow in 1991, it was seen on television by Western leaders, who immediately recognized his political strength at the time. When a lone student confronted a tank in Tiananmen Square, the world watched him and felt the tensions in Beijing, colouring political attitudes towards China around the globe.

Once the media began carrying their words, politicians had to face the reality that they could no longer get away with outrageous comments designed to sway a particular audience. In the United States, for instance, politicians could no longer make the kind of charges uttered by senatorial candidate George Smathers in his 1950 Florida primary campaign against veteran Democrat Claude Pepper. The newspapers and *Time* magazine reported Smathers telling unsophisticated rural Floridians in a shocked tone, "Are you aware that Claude Pepper is known all over Washington as a shameless extrovert? Not only that, but this man is reliably reported to practice nepotism with his sister-in-law, and he has a sister who was once a thespian in wicked New York. Worst of all, it is an established fact that Mr. Pepper before his marriage habitually practiced celibacy." The good Floridians apparently were properly shocked, rejected Pepper, and elected Smathers to the senate.

While radio and TV enormously enlarged the audience for what statesmen and politicians said, in its day so, too, did the Penny Press of the nineteenth century. Benjamin Disraeli and William Gladstone, Sir John A. Macdonald and Sir Wilfrid Laurier all knew that because of the lengthening reach of journalism provided by technology, they had to address themselves to a much larger audience in their later days than in their earlier days. Similarly, today's leaders in Ottawa, Washington, and Moscow face ever-larger audiences who get information immediately when something happens.

The media of the late 1990s are profoundly different from the media of the 1970s because of the ferocious competitive pressures brought by twenty-four-hour TV news and the Internet. Every second is a deadline, pressing reporters on big, breaking stories to rush into print, on air, or onto the Web with whatever news they have. The rush gives them little time for thought, and all too often they break news without double- and triple-checking their information with unconnected sources and without getting reaction from those involved. At the CBC, there is an ironclad rule about double-checking with unconnected sources in investigative journalism. It proved invaluable, for instance, in uncovering the scandal in 1977 over RCMP illegal break-ins, phone tapping, mail openings, barn burnings, and other misdeeds. Double- and triple-checking facts means it takes longer before a story goes to air, but the plodding detail work of investigative reporting is absolutely essential in getting to the truth and in protecting journalistic integrity. As head of news and current-affairs programming for CBC-TV at the time, I was proud of the standards followed by our Ottawa reporters, and could confidently refute government complaints about the revelations of RCMP transgressions.

The media's traditional scepticism began climbing in the United States in President Lyndon Johnson's day. Journalists labelled him "Lyin' Lyndon" for his dissembling about Vietnam and his lack of credibility. We Washington reporters joked at the time that the Texas-reared Johnson lived in "Credibility Gap" and when asked where that was, replied, "You go west until you smell it, then go south until you step in it."

This media sarcasm went into high gear with President Richard Nixon's lying about Watergate, giving weight to his nickname, "Tricky Dick." By the mid-1970s, journalists, having been lied to so much, began shifting from scepticism to cynicism about government officials, and their reporting became more accusatory than explanatory.

While Canadian reporters are not nearly so aggressive as their American colleagues, they are propelled by the same technological competition and the same cynicism. One result is a more distant relationship between politicians and reporters than was true in the 1950s and '60s and a rule of thumb that nothing is off the record any more. That was forcefully brought home in our 1984 federal election campaign. At one point during the campaign, Tory leader Brian Mulroney joked with reporters about Liberal patronage appointments but was appalled when he saw in print his off-the-record comment that "There's no whore like an old whore." Similarly, Prime Minister John Turner was shocked when his off-the-cuff remarks about why he quit the Trudeau cabinet became front-page news. The relationship between politicians and journalists had changed dramatically, and Turner, Mulroney, and their colleagues had to change, too.

Knowing that whatever they say may be used, politicians have become much more cautious in talking to reporters informally, and I'm not persuaded this is helpful in the job of informing the public. Even in so-called private conversations with journalists, politicians today are carefully protective of the image they want to project. Sometimes I frankly long for the days when political leaders could climb down from their public pedestals to have a relaxed, down-to-earth conversation with a journalist. The journalist did not report on the substance of these conversations, but knowing what a politician truly thought about this or that would inform the journalist's reports and analysis. While I agree with Walter Lippmann's comment that journalists "cannot be the cronies of great men," I think journalists and, through them, the public can benefit from an acquaintanceship between reporters and great men and women.

I was able to get a good sense of the man and his purpose in chatting off the record in hotel rooms, airplanes, or at his home with John F. Kennedy when he was a senator and a presidential candidate. It was a different world from today's, for while there was gossip aplenty among reporters and a few knowing winks from Kennedy himself in private conversations, none of us at the time pursued his sex life as a news story. We focused instead on the job he did as president and assumed, as was the then current discipline, that his sex life was private.

Although I didn't report what was said, I'm persuaded that the knowledge I gained from personal encounters with Kennedy and others made my reports richer and better informed on the public issues he was dealing with. I learned, for instance, that he thought John Diefenbaker was "a liar," "a blackmailer," and a "betrayer." Once, while we were paddling about in his swimming pool at his home outside Washington, Bobby Kennedy told me in graphic detail how much his brother despised Diefenbaker. "My brother really hated only two men in his life. One was Sukarno [the dictator of Indonesia] and the other was Diefenbaker," he told me. While I didn't quote him at the time, knowing in detail the testiness of the relationship was useful in reporting on Canada–U.S. issues.

Similarly, I found it journalistically rewarding to attend private, informal discussions with Lyndon Johnson. I got to know the earthy nature of the man, so different from his public pose. From such meetings, I could better read between the lines of politicians' public actions and comments. Also off the record and valuable were sessions with senior-level government officials, especially at the State Department. There were three types of sessions: background, deep background, and deep deep background. In background discussions, as a reporter you could say that a State Department official said such and such. On deep background, you could only say, "An American official said . . ." On deep deep background, you could only say it was understood the government felt this way or that about an issue.

The latter stories were called "thumb suckers" because they appeared speculative as there was no indication of the source, although our editors were told who the source was.

A variation of deep deep background is where the ground rules going in are that nothing is for quotation, but if the reporter later wants to use a quote, it's negotiable.

The writer and observer of contemporary society A. J. Liebling once noted somewhat sardonically the differences among reporters, observers, and experts. A reporter, he said, is someone who goes somewhere and tells you what's going on. An observer, he continued, is someone who goes somewhere and tells you what it means. An expert, he concluded, is someone who goes nowhere and tells you what everything means.

The media are the linchpin between the governed and the governors. Media outlets – whether print, broadcast, or the Internet – are the only way politicians have to get their message to the public at large. Similarly, the media are the only way the public can send messages back to their governments, except at election time or in revolution. But the media have another obligation, and that is to search for the truth. At the trial of Jesus Christ, Pontius Pilate asked, "What is truth?" and that's the central question for which, two thousand years later, journalists must find an answer, for journalism is all about seeking the truth.

3

From Drums to Cyberspace

"All men by nature desire knowledge," said the Greek philosopher Aristotle. In seeking knowledge, we've distributed news by drums, smoke signals, gongs, satellites, and a web of connected computers. Cavemen grunted news of the day around fires and Athenians exchanged news in the Agora. Humans began making images and keeping records more than twenty-five thousand years ago. Five thousand years ago, the Neolithic villagers living near Xi'an in central China were drawing pictures of events in their everyday lives. The first known written news was inscribed about 3500 B.C. on Sumerian clay tablets in pictorial symbols of battles.

The clash we face today between news as entertainment and news as enlightenment was evident at the beginning. Mesopotamian scribes wrote stories about adultery in a "trysting house" and of robberies. Around 1500 B.C., a group of Mesopotamian tablets inscribed in cuneiform script exposed a corruption scandal in the town of Nuzu. The mayor was accused of theft, extortion, and having sexual intercourse with a married woman. The report included the mayor's denial. Egyptian scribes wrote in clay and later on dried papyrus leaves, and in 1100 B.C. they reported on the torture of thieves who had confessed to plundering the tomb of Pharaoh Ramses the Great. One of the thieves was quoted as saying, "We tore off the gold that we found."

News was important to the ancient Egyptians. Their scribe for the gods, Thoth, was a searcher for truth and a "master of word." He is said to have appeared in human form with the head of an ibis, or as contemporary media critics might think, as a dog-faced baboon. A millennium or so later, Romans were reading a daily gazette known as *Urbana Acta*, which reported government statements, debate in the senate, news of war, and gossip.

The *Roman Gazette* was posted at the Forum and other central points in Rome, and it or other Roman newssheets lasted from about the middle of the first century B.C. to the dying days of the empire in the fifth century A.D. It was copied by hand and sent off to officials and the élite in the provinces of the empire, which in its heyday stretched from northern England to southern Egypt.

In addition to official news, crime, and scandal, Roman scribes writing on Egyptian papyrus included in their reports heart-warming features such as the tale of a dog that wouldn't leave his dead master's side and jumped into the Tiber River to follow his body.

Even in ancient Rome, some objected to there being too much entertainment in the news. Cicero, who was an avid reader of the *Gazette* and other news reports in 51 B.C. when he was proconsul of Cilicia in what is now southern Turkey, was one who complained. His Roman colleague, Caelius, sent him detailed reports on "Decrees of the Senate, edicts, rumours" and included items of gossip on marriages, divorces, and adultery. Caelius, however, disliked the junk news, and told Cicero, "There is much which you must skip." Cicero himself complained of too much "gladiatorial pairs," "adjournment of trials," "burglary," and too much "tittle-tattle." Pliny the Elder was also a complainer about the news in the first century A.D., saying that the *Gazette* reported too much on crime, fires, and divorces.

About the same time the Romans were reading the *Gazette*, the Chinese were sending a handwritten newsletter, or *Tipau*, to outlying provinces to sustain the power of the Han Dynasty. The *Tipau* was written for the eyes of the élite, as Chinese leaders at the time followed Confucius's advice to keep their subjects uninformed. The *Tipau* was prepared by a Bureau of Official Reports and reported on edicts, promotions, dismissals, and deaths. One of the biggest news stories related in the *Tipau* happened in 138 B.C. when an emissary from Emperor Wudi discovered the kingdoms of central Asia and learned of the existence of Rome, Persia, and India. It was news as big in its day as Columbus's discovery of America.

Strict government controls kept out any sensationalist reporting in the *Tipau*. It wasn't until centuries later with the much wider circulation of private newsletters and small newspapers, or *Hsiaopao*, that concern arose in China over "tittle-tattle" news. One newsletter report, complete with vivid eyewitness accounts, was on the execution of a bandit leader named Huang Chao, whose head was chopped off "and sent to Xichua." During the Sung Dynasty in the twelfth century A.D., a Chinese official named Chou Linchih warned the emperor that "sensationalist news" was "misleading the public." This, he said, was "injurious to the administration and demands our attention. I humbly petition that Your Majesty should issue an edict prohibiting their circulation." The emperor immediately began censoring private as well as government newsletters to eliminate sensationalism.

Most people, whether in the Roman Empire or China, did not have access to written news since few of them could read. Even so, the collapse of the Roman Empire led to a decline in literacy throughout Europe and there was a consequent shrivelling of the flow of written news. It wasn't until the Renaissance that handwritten newssheets again began moving along the routes of the old *Roman Gazette*.

Until then, for the vast majority, knowledge of what was happening came through verbal distribution of the news by balladeers. People heard rather than read the news, much as happens today now that print has lost its dominance to the balladeers of broadcasting such as Peter Mansbridge, Lloyd Robertson, Peter Jennings, Dan Rather, and Tom Brokaw.

Moving from town to town, spreading the news to the pre-literate masses, the balladeers of the Middle Ages featured far more gossip and sensationalism and were less accurate than the handwritten newssheets. As Mitchell Stephens reports in his book *A History of News*, one of the most prominent English news balladeers of the late 1500s was Thomas Deloney, known as "The Ballating Silke Weaver [his former job] of Norwich [who] hath rime inough for all myracles." In one of his news ballads, he reported on the defeat of the Spanish Armada, singing, "And manie more, by sword did loose their breath, and manie more within the sea, did swimme and took their death." He also sang a report about "the strange and most cruel Whippes which the Spanyards had prepared to whippe and torment English men and women."

News balladeers of the 1500s also sought out news from their listeners, singing, "What newes? Or here ye any tidinges of the Pope, of the Emperor, or of kynges. Or of Martin Luther, of the great Turke, of this and that and how the world doth worke."

In Asia, there was the Mongolian Telegraph, horsemen galloping between towns spreading the news, just as the Pony Express would do centuries later in the American West. Zulu tribesmen and Amerindians had criers who, like the European and Asian news criers, owed their allegiance to tribal and community leaders.

But, as in Roman days and as is the case today, there was concern in the Middle Ages about too much sensationalism in the news ballads. In the 1440s, King Richard III admonished citizens against "the telling of tales and tidings whereby the people might be stirred to commocions."

English officials in the Middle Ages were concerned about "lewd" news ballads and "corrupted tales" being sung in towns and villages throughout the kingdom. One ballad was entitled "Tydings of a huge and ougly childe burnt at Arnhem in Gelderland." Others told of "the birth of three monsters in the city of Namen in Flanders" or "The Strange and Miraculous revelation of a murder by a ghost, a calf, a pigeon, etc." in Lancashire. The roots of the sensationalism in today's *National Enquirer*, *Star*, or *Globe* are indeed deep.

An English news ballad in 1616 recorded the tale of five men who drowned while attempting to cross the Thames River. "But being all with drinke growne madd, they were in wofull manner drownd," the balladeers sang. Mitchell Stephens notes that a 1635 news ballad reported the hanging of a man and a woman who had murdered three people. The woman, "a filthy whore," corrupted her lover, the ballad claimed. He was "a man of honest parentage," but "she sotted his mind," and they lived a "vile loose life."

Women were frequently portrayed as villainesses in news ballads. One described a woman, thirty years older than her husband, who stabbed him because "she was not a little tainted with the passion of Jealousie." Another news ballad told of a French woman who killed her English husband and dismembered his body after she had contracted venereal disease from him. He had, the ballad reported, forced her into "a compliance with him in Villainies contrary to nature."

Although they reached far fewer people than the balladeers, handwritten newsletters and newsbooks of four to twenty-five pages would be passed from hand to hand or tacked up on posts in European cities throughout the fourteenth and fifteenth centuries. But even with as many as fifty copyists working in what were called "writing shops," newsletters and newsbooks stayed out of reach of the masses until one of the greatest technological developments in information dissemination ever invented, the printing press, came along. The printed word spurred a rise in literacy and more people turned to the written word for the news.

Printed news began dominating news delivery and did so for five hundred years, until television news reclaimed the dominance of verbal news dissemination in the late twentieth century.

China entered the print era first, developing the technique of block printing to reproduce documents in the T'ang Dynasty of 618–907 A.D. Paper also was developed by the Chinese in 105 A.D., and one thousand years later it reached Europe. Movable clay type was developed in China in 1000 A.D. and metal type in the 1400s. A form of printing developed in Europe in the late thirteenth century in which a page was printed by rubbing a sheet of paper against inked blocks of wood, carved to produce the impression of words and pictures. This kind of printing existed half a century before the German Johannes Gutenberg developed his printing press, using movable metal type, about 1436. Like many future printers, however, Gutenberg went broke and had to give up his press and type to pay off his debts. Within fifty years, however, presses were running in more than 235 cities and towns throughout Europe.

Gutenberg's first print job was a run of two hundred copies of the Bible, and soon his invention was revolutionizing European society. By 1500, half a million Bibles had been printed. Martin Luther said the Protestant Reformation couldn't have happened without the printing press.

Beyond giving people access to the Bible for the first time, printing and paper provided the ability for the news to reach much of Europe within days instead of months. The early printing was done on sheets made from rags or hide parchment, both of which were expensive. It took, for instance, the skins of two hundred to three hundred sheep or calves to provide enough parchment to print a Bible. Canadian technology writer Wade Rowland has noted in his book *Spirit of the Web* that rags for paper were so scarce that in the nineteenth century, Egyptian mummies were imported to the United States so that the linen in which the mummies were wrapped could be recycled to make paper. Paper made from wood pulp was developed about 1860. Because of its low price, wood-based paper helped fuel the vast increase in newspaper circulation.

The availability of printed newssheets in the 1500s meant the news could begin to be read by ordinary people as well as by the élite, although at the time about 90 per cent of

Europeans were still illiterate. The idea of the public at large having access to information on events, however, was viewed dimly by many in the élite. They had had a monopoly on learning and felt that bringing knowledge to the masses endangered their power and degraded the value of learning. Four hundred years after Gutenberg, that view persisted among some, including the German philosopher Friedrich Nietzsche, who said, "Everyone being allowed to read ruineth in the long run not only writing but also thinking." This sentiment was reminiscent of the concerns of some early Egyptian scholars who felt writing would "implant forgetfulness" and people would "cease to exercise memory." Later, even Socrates and Plato were uneasy about the value of writing.

Because of the enlarged potential readership, early publishers of printed news, like most contemporary publishers, were concerned with being popular. While they printed extended articles on the activities of royalty, of politicians, of the economy, and of foreign affairs, much of their emphasis was on "soft features." The printed news was generally shorter, less detailed, even less thoughtful than the articles in many handwritten newsletters.

One of the most successful of the printed newsletters of the late 1500s was produced by a German financial institution with wide contacts throughout Europe, the House of Fugger. The Fugger newsletter reported battles, plots, births, deaths, and other events. Although it was designed for merchants, traders, and political leaders, it also provided sensational news. A 1592 edition reported from Saragossa, Spain, "Don Juan de Luna had his head cut off from the front and Don Diego from the back. Ayerbe and Dionysio Perez merely had their throats cut, then they were laid down and left to die by inches. Pedro de Fuerdes, they strangled with a rope. When he was dead he was quartered and the four quarters hung out in the streets of Saragossa."

In 1575, an English newsletter reported "loose desire" and "foul lust" leading to murder. Reporting became more vivid over the years: a news story in 1624, headlined "The Crying Murther. Contayning the Cruell and Most Horrible Butcher of Mr. Trat," read, ". . . these butchers, with their hands already smoking in his blood, did cut up his carcass, unbowel and quarter it, then did they burn his head and privy members, parboil his flesh and salt it up . . . his arms, legs, thighs, and bowels were powdered up into two earthen steens or ports in a lower room of the house . . . the bulk of his carcass was placed in a vat or tub."

Complete with vivid drawings, a 1637 English newsletter headlined a story about two women who were executed for murdering their own children: "Natures Cruell Step-dames or Matchless Monsters of the Female Sex." There was more sex and violence in the same newsletter with a front-page report on "The wicked life and impenitent death of John Flood who raped his own childe." A woman in Kent was reported in an 1655 edition of the *Weekly Intelligence of the Commonwealth* to have killed her husband's lover and then cooked and served him his lover's vulva.

As it does today, murder fascinated early journalists, as witness this 1598 English headline: "The Examination, Confession and Condemnation of Henry Robson, Fisherman of Rye Who Poysoned His Wife in the Strangest Manner Than Ever Hitherto Hath Bin Heard Of." A 1605 newsbook story recounted the tale of "pittilesse" Sir John Fites, who was "thirstie of bloud" and who killed a man, stabbed the man's wife, and then fell on his own sword.

Freaks and horrors were as prominent in the news then as they are in today's supermarket tabloids. An English report covered the story of "A Strange and Monstrous Serpant (or Dragon)" living in the Sussex forest thirty miles from London. A German story told of a monster seen in Spain with "goat legs, a human body, seven arms and seven heads." There was another report of a nine-foot dragon spitting flames and killing people. In 1576, a French news report, offering what it called "Horribles Detailes," described a "Monstrous and frightful serpant" with two heads and wings. Another story reported a dragon flying over Paris. Still another newsletter in 1562 reported a monster with "neyther hande, foote, legge, nor arme, but on the left syde it hath a stumpe growynge out of the shoulder."

Even royalty was also intrigued with sensationalist news. The Russian tsars of the seventeenth century, for example, were given newssheets with a section entitled "Curiosa – the strange and unusual."

Even in the 1600s, the murders, the sensationalism, the freak and horror stories in the popular press aroused the scorn of the élite. Ballads were described as "filthy" and "indecent," news-books and newsletters were denounced as "mere shreds and tatters of sensation." "Trifles, pieces of nonsense, fables, frivolities, drolleries, charlatanries and pranks" were epithets hurled at newsbooks by the seventeenth-century French writer Pierre de l'Estoile. The seventeenth-century English censor and writer Sir Roger L'Estrange worried that the sensationalism of newsletters and newsbooks might lead to people being "juggled out of the Senses with so many Frightful Stories."

Underground French newspapers of the late 1700s also often catered to circulation-building sensationalism. In Paris, one paper described Queen Marie Antoinette masturbating and claimed King Louis XVI was impotent. Another paper reported that Marie Antoinette had been impregnated by a cardinal. Earlier, Madame Du Barry, mistress of King Louis XV, was accused of passing "directly from the Brothel to the Throne," and the king himself was reported to "consume" two different girls a week besides his wife and mistress.

In 1616, there was an official complaint in Oxford that scholarly work was being neglected and "nothing but news and the affairs of Christendome is discussed." Oxford became a hotbed of news after the first coffee house in England opened in that city around 1650. Tradesmen, politicians, soldiers, workers came to these shops to sip coffee and exchange news and gossip. There was so much news, the coffee houses began specializing, with some featuring only political news, others only military news, or news of the theatre, scholarship, or trade, a specialization not dissimilar to the late twentieth-century specialization by TV cable channels and magazines. In the coffee houses, however, there was always also a large dose of crime news, gossip, and scandal.

By the early 1700s in London, there were hundreds of news-dispensing coffee houses charging a penny a cup. The French began news distribution in coffee houses about the same time as the British, and in India there were tea shops where the news was exchanged. The coffee houses attracted eavesdropping "news boys" or "spectators for hire," who worked for newsletters and weekly papers. Their presence was not totally welcome, as reflected in one critical newsletter article: "Persons are employed (One or Two for each Paper) at so much a week to haunt Coffee Houses and thrust themselves into companies where they are not known, or plant themselves at a convenient Distance to overhear what is said, in order to pick up Matter for the Paper." The article also complained about "news boys" picking up gossip from footmen, clerks, and servants of the nobility and gentry. "The same Persons hang and loiter about the Publick Offices like Housebreakers, waiting for an Interview with some little clerk or a conference with a Door Keeper in order to come at a little News." That sounds a bit like Woodward and Bernstein chasing their Watergate story by talking to Washington secretaries and office clerks.

The first newspaper, as distinct from newsletters and newsbooks, was printed in Strasbourg in 1609, a four-page weekly called *Relation* and aimed at the rich and powerful. It featured both serious and trivial news. One story reported on a discovery by Galileo and another on a general who had been forbidden to play ninepins. Over the next few decades, newspapers (a word that historian Mitchell Stephens notes didn't come into use until about 1670) were launched in Frankfurt, Vienna, Berlin, Amsterdam, Paris, Rome, and London. The first English newspaper, published in 1620, had the same problems that affect today's papers when reporters miss their deadlines. It noted that "the new tydings out of Italie are not yet com." The first daily newspaper began in Germany in 1650, but it was another fifty years before a daily paper appeared in England.

Merchants and traders of the time were particularly avid readers of newspapers and newsletters because, with early knowledge of events, they could increase trade profits. Venetian merchants in the early sixteenth century, for example, wanted news of ships carrying spices from India. If ships were sunk or lost, the price of spices would zoom, so the sooner a trader had the news, the more profit he could make. A century or two later, grain traders who got early news of a drop in wheat harvests would move quickly to profit from the impending shortage and resultant higher prices. In 1815, Nathan Rothschild received early news of Napoleon's defeat at Waterloo and made a fortune on the London Stock Exchange, buying at low prices before British investors heard of the victory.

Sensationalism and drama gained prominence in the newspapers when editors, most of whom were also owners, began vying for greater circulation. The twice-weekly *London Gazette* was established in 1665, and within a few years London boasted twenty papers appearing weekly, twice weekly, or three times a week. They also were hiring reporters, calling them "matter of fact men," and a few women journalists also were hired, known as "she intelligencers."

A story in the London newspaper *A Perfect Diurnall* on the execution of King Charles I in 1649 reflected a new style of reporting. It noted on page three: "Tuesday, January 30, This day the King was beheaded, over against the Banquetting house by White Hall." Demonstrating a flair for dramatic detail, the paper described the execution: "Then the King, speaking to the executioner, said, 'I shall say but very short prayer and then thrust out my hands.' The king then said, to the executioner, 'Is my hair well?' Then the King took off his cloak . . . then looking upon the block, said, to the executioner, 'You must set it fast.'

"Executioner: 'It is fast, sir.'

"King: 'It might have been a little higher.'

"Executioner: 'It can be no higher sir.'

"After that, having said two or three words (as he stood) to himself, with hands and eyes lifted up; immediately stooping down, laid his neck upon the block . . . and after a very little pause, the King stretched forth his hands. The Executioner at one blow severed his head from his body . . . When the King's head was cut off, the Executioner held it up and showed it to the spectators."

This kind of journalistic drama made the papers "more vendable," said a seventeenth-century writer. In 1679, editor Benjamin Harris gave much prominence to murderous details in a story of a man found hanging "by the arms in a wood . . . with his head and hands cut off and his Bowels pulled out."

Early American newspapers also used sensationalism as a circulation builder. In fact, the same scandal-loving British editor, Benjamin Harris, used sensationalism and human misery to make a dramatic impact when he published the first newspaper in North America in Boston in 1690. In his paper, *Publick Occurrences Both Foreign and Domestic*, Harris cited a report that the king of France used to lie "with his son's wife." He also reported on a man hanging himself in the "cow house" and in another story reported on the "miserable savages" threatening the lives of American settlers. Harris's first issue of *Publick Occurrences* was his last. Colonial authorities shut down his paper, saying it contained "sundry doubtful and uncertain reports." The British colonial authorities in London advised the Massachusetts governor that "great inconvenience may arise by the liberty of printing." But by 1730, there were seven regularly published papers in the American colonies, and by 1800 more than 180, most of which did indeed give the authorities "great inconvenience."

By then, however, the American Revolution had been won and the ferociously opinionated American press turned its aggressiveness on its own with sensational denunciations of politicians. Journalistic attacks on American presidents certainly didn't start with the exposés of Bill Clinton's allegedly superactive libido. George Washington read newspaper accounts of his alleged womanizing, an illegitimate son, corruption, swindling, and general "debauchery." He also was accused of being an "atrocious wretch," of military incompetence, and of stealing $5,000 from the Continental Army. The second American president, John Adams, was accused by one newspaper of "unbounded thirst for ridiculous pomp, foolish adulation or selfish avarice." Newspapers trumpeted charges that Thomas Jefferson's mistress was a black slave. Andrew Johnson was labelled a drunk and accused of living with a woman not legally his wife. Grover Cleveland suffered even more media assault than Bill Clinton as newspapers accused Cleveland of being an inebriated philanderer. "A Drunken, Fighting, Roistering Roue," headlined the *Cincinnati Penny Post.*

Charges of sexual misbehaviour against presidents have echoed through the years not only against Washington, Jefferson, Johnson, and Cleveland, but also against Chester Arthur, Andrew Jackson, Abraham Lincoln, Woodrow Wilson, Warren Harding, Franklin Delano Roosevelt, Dwight Eisenhower, John F. Kennedy, Lyndon Johnson, George Bush, and Bill Clinton. James Buchanan, the only bachelor president, was accused of being a homosexual, and James Garfield, although married, was accused of having homosexual flings.

Early Canadian prime ministers were not assailed by the media to the same degree as their U.S. counterparts. Sir John A.

Macdonald's drinking was certainly made fun of, but Canadian newspapers of the 1800s tended to be less salacious than the American press, more interested in politics than in sleaze.

The most scurrilous and licentious English news reporting came from what became known as the Grub Street Press, whose hack writers specialized in scandal. The *Grub Street Journal* (1730–39) epitomized the shocking and titillating London popular press of those days with its emphasis on murder, rape, scandal, fires, and robbery. The Grub Street type of newspaper may have been widely read by ordinary people, but it was despised by the élites, who feared this kind of low-class journalism endangered intelligent discourse. The press, said eighteenth-century writer Samuel Johnson, has "too little to enlarge the mind." A British MP of the late 1700s, William Windham, complained that the press treated politicians like actors. "What was to become of the dignity of the House," he asked, "if the manners and gestures and tone and action of each member were to be the subject to the license, the abuse, the ribaldry of newspapers?"

British philosopher and economist John Stuart Mill said of the reporters of the 1800s, "Our daily and weekly writers are the lowest of literature which, when it is a trade, is the vilest and most degrading of all trades." Friedrich Nietzsche said, "They vomit up their bile and call it a newspaper." In 1777, a preacher named William Dodd on trial for forgery was accused in court of having "descended so low as to become the editor of a newspaper." All this was not too far from Conrad Black's twentieth-century comment that investigative journalists are "swarming, grunting masses of jackals."

But Grub Street had found a format for success and didn't

care what epithets were hurled. The *Two Penny Dispatch*, which began in London in 1834, promised its readers that the paper would be "a repository of all the gems and treasures and fun and frolic and news and occurrences of the week. It shall abound in Police Intelligence, in Murders, Rapes, Suicides, Burnings, Maimings, Theatricals, Races, Pugilism and all manner of moving accidents by flood and field. In short, it will be stuffed with every sort of devilment that will make it sell." And sell it did; two years later, it had a circulation of 27,000, an impressively high figure for those days especially when compared to the circulation of less than 10,000 of the much more sober *London Times*, which provided lengthy political and economic articles, parliamentary debates, reports of activities of the ruling classes, and diplomatic happenings from abroad.

But there was an underlying political purpose to much of the Fleet Street sensationalism. By the 1800s, the popular press was using sensationalism to sugar-coat radical politics. In a way, Fleet Street was following the guidance of St. Thomas Aquinas, who urged the theatrical use of imagery to convey understanding. "All knowledge has its origins in sensation," he said. One man who pursued that approach was a journalist by the name of Charles Dickens. In 1835, he was a scoop-chasing reporter for the *London Morning Chronicle*, whose stories seethed with the injustice of poverty, crime, and politics. Dickens was not, however, a believer in journalistic impartiality. Reporting an election in which his favoured Liberals lost, Dickens wrote that the loss could be blamed on "the most ignorant, drunken and brutal electors in these Kingdoms who have been treated and fed and driven up to the polls the whole day like herds of swine."

Dickens was a rabble-rousing reporter, sympathetic to the downtrodden, outraged at the idle rich, and appalled by authoritarianism. In search of stories, he accompanied the police on their nightly patrols, and his sensationalism and sentimentalism is seen in one 1851 report of visiting a poor house: "We open [the door] and are stricken back by the pestilent breath that issues from within. . . . Ten, twenty, thirty – who can count them. Men, women, children, for the most part naked, heaped upon the floor like maggots in a cheese."

Competition then, as now, was fierce among reporters as they tried to outdo their opposition by bribing officials, shooting down each other's news-carrying pigeons, and occasionally hijacking each other's trains and stagecoaches.

In the mid-1800s, there was a newspaper boom after Britain abolished a century-old stamp tax, which had been aimed at limiting the popular press by imposing a tax on each sheet of paper. Soon rapidly spreading literacy, flowing from new laws about compulsory education, added to the boom in the Penny Press. In 1800, half of Europe was still illiterate, but this was down to a tenth by 1900. As a critic at the time commented, "Scarce a cat can look out of the gutter but starts a half penny chronicler." Circulations jumped to the tens of thousands. The *Weekly Police Gazette* began in 1834 charging one penny and had an initial circulation of 20,000. A decade later, the *News of the World* began providing, also for a penny, a basic recipe of saucy scandal, crime, and anti-rich exposés, just as it does today. The *Black Dwarf*, using a similar formula, had a circulation of 12,000 in the 1840s. Higher circulations were helped by the invention of the steam press. In 1814, the *Times of London* could print 1,100 copies an hour and, by 1837, the *Sun* in New York was printing 4,000 copies an hour.

As the 1800s wore on, the Sunday mass-circulation papers became increasingly both influential and profitable. *Lloyd's Weekly Newspaper* in London was the first to go over a million in circulation near the end of the century. More than 50 per cent of the paper was devoted to robberies, scandal, murder, and gossip and only 15 to 20 per cent was devoted to serious journalism such as stories about politics, the economy, or royal activities.

Alfred Harmsworth, the future press baron Lord Northcliffe, founded his newspaper empire with *Answers to Correspondents*, a trivia-possessed paper whose headlines included "Do Dogs Commit Murder?" "Why Jews Don't Ride Bicycles," or "Can Fish Speak?" His theory was that no news article should be longer than 250 words, and his motto was "All the news in sixty seconds." When Harmsworth established the *Daily Mail* in London, which was only a cut or two above *Answers*, Prime Minister Lord Salisbury sniffed disdainfully, saying the *Daily Mail* was "a newspaper for office boys, written by office boys." Even so, papers such as the *Mail* made political powerhouses out of the likes of Northcliffe (who was known as "The Napoleon of Fleet Street"), Rothermere, and, later, Beaverbrook.

The radical press tended to be more sensational in part because it needed the income from selling more papers since advertisers were less supportive than they were of the quality papers. The success of the formula of sensational reportage, lampoons, and soak-the-rich politics alarmed the élites, who condemned what they called the "radical press" as a danger to the country's stability. It might lead, Prime Minister Lord Salisbury warned, to empowering the poor and a situation in which "the rich would pay all the taxes and the poor would make all the laws."

The first Canadian news publication was a newssheet published in Halifax in 1752 called the *Halifax Gazette*, which began with a circulation of seventy-two copies. In New France, the printing press was late in coming because French colonial officials feared it would undermine their authority. After the British Conquest, the first Quebec paper, the *Quebec Gazette*, was established in 1764 by two Philadelphia printers. A hundred and forty-three copies of its initial edition were sold. It survives today as the *Quebec Chronicle-Telegraph*. At the end of the 1700s, more newspapers were born in Halifax, in Charlottetown, Saint John, Montreal, and in Upper Canada, and by the mid-1830s there were nearly fifty newspapers in Canada. The Montreal *Gazette* is Canada's oldest, continually published daily paper. While not as flashy as much of the British and American press, Canadian papers carried a tinge of sensationalism with stories of two-headed cows, African cannibals, mad dogs, and "Murder and Arson in the Indian Country," as reported by the Toronto *Patriot*.

Unlike the Canadian papers or newspapers of London's Fleet Street, the sensation-hungry press of the United States in the 1800s used flash-and-trash journalism more for profit than political purposes.

Typical of that approach was James Gordon Bennett, whose brazen reports pushed the New York *Herald* to a daily circulation of 20,000 a year after he launched the paper in 1835. Bennett, who had been one of the first Washington correspondents, not only was a newspaper owner, but also became the first American investigative reporter. Characteristic of his supercharged approach was his reporting of the axe murder of a young prostitute. Under the headline "The Horrible Murder of Miss Jewitt," Bennett wrote, "He [the murderer] then drew from beneath his cloak the hatchet and inflicted upon her head three blows, either of which must have proved fatal as the bone was cleft to the extent of three inches in each place." For days Bennett's purple reports on this story captivated readers, as did the excerpts from the girl's love letters that he'd found. Circulation soared. It also soared during stunts such as, in 1869, sending reporter Henry Morton Stanley to Africa to find Dr. David Livingstone. While in Africa, Stanley was accused of starting several little wars among tribesmen and then reporting on them.

Trying to undercut the *Herald* and also focusing on sensationalism was the New York *Sun*, sold for a penny and boasting a circulation of 15,000 with a lively mix of crime, human-interest stories, accidents, and scandals. Challenging the *Herald* in flamboyance, the *Sun* said its aim was "diverting the public mind." Once, it reported that creatures on the moon had been discovered by a new telescope based in South Africa, splashing the story on its front page. "They averaged four feet in height, were covered, except on the face, with short and glossy copper hair, and had wings composed of membranes," the paper said. The *Sun*'s circulation leapt. Only later did the newspaper admit it was all a hoax. The old journalistic bromide, when dog bites man, that's not news, but when man bites dog, that *is* news, originated about this time in the editorial rooms of the *Sun*.

The closest American newspapers came to the mix of sensationalism and politics of the English popular press was Joseph Pulitzer's New York *World*. His journalistic exploitation of crime, human misery, and scandal was matched with crusading, progressive politics. With this formula he pushed the *World*'s daily circulation from about 15,000 when he took over the paper in 1883 to 190,000, and 250,000 on Sundays by 1887.

If ever there was a prize for trash news, however, it would go to a one-time reporter for Bennett, William Randolph Hearst.

The son of a silver baron, Hearst saw the potential for profit in sensationalism and launched his own papers, although with less intelligence and more belligerence than either Bennett or, especially, Pulitzer. "The public is even more fond of entertainment than it is of information," Hearst said after buying the New York *Journal* in 1895. In a slam at Hearst, the more responsible but less popular *New York Times* advertised at the time, "To be seen reading the *New York Times* is a stamp of respectability," and its slogan was "All the world's news but not a school for scandal." A U.S. senate report in 1928 characterized Hearst's record as "the blackest in American journalism."

But none of that inhibited Hearst's buccaneering manner. There was no more vivid example of Hearst's exploitative style than the Spanish–American War, which he almost single-handedly started as a circulation builder for his newspapers, blaming Spain on the flimsiest of evidence for, among other things, sinking the battleship *Maine* in Havana Harbour. Through his New York *Journal*, he aroused public passions with horror stories and successfully pressured the U.S. government to attack the Spanish in Cuba. One of Hearst's news artists on the scene in Cuba before hostilities broke out, the great illustrator Frederic Remington, cabled Hearst that he wanted to leave because war seemed unlikely. Hearst cabled back, "Please remain. You furnish pictures. I will furnish war." One of his reporters, Canadian-born James Creelman, even led a bayonet charge. At one point, with his sensational stories, Hearst's New York *Journal* sold 3 million copies in three days.

Hearst's formula of jingoism and sensationalism propelled him into being the most powerful publisher in the United States. At its height, his journalistic empire included twenty daily papers, eleven Sunday papers, two international news agencies, the largest news feature syndicate in the United States, a newsreel company, and a motion picture studio. When Hearst spoke, even Franklin Delano Roosevelt listened.

The circulation battles between Hearst and Pulitzer encouraged gutter journalism. They also fought over the ownership of the first popular comic strip, "The Yellow Kid," which lampooned the upper class. Because both newspapers were such fulsome practitioners of sensational reporting, part of the comic strip title was used to describe their news style, which became known as "yellow" journalism. The American writer and satirist Ambrose Bierce castigated the Yellow Press, saying they were "newspapers conducted by rogues and dunces for dunces and rogues. . . . They fetter the feet of wisdom and stiffen the prejudices of the ignorant. They are sycophants to the mob, tyrants to the individual." Another characterization that also connoted sensationalism was "tabloid," a name that fittingly originated in the 1880s in the United States as a trade name for a compressed, easy-to-digest pill and was applied to small-format newspapers with big and exciting headlines.

Near the end of the 1800s, there was a graphic example of the New York newspaper rivalries and circulation wars. Lincoln Steffens, one of the early, great American investigative reporters, single-handedly created a serious crime wave in New York City. Covering the police beat for the New York *Evening Post*, he wrote an exclusive story of a burglary at the home of a prominent Wall Street broker. Competing police reporters, stung by his scoop, discovered a number of other burglaries about which the police had not bothered to advise them. Soon crime stories were sweeping the New York front pages. New Yorkers became alarmed, editorials thundered about laxity in the police department, and businesses selling locks, guard dogs, and other crime-prevention devices boomed. It became a political issue because the "crime wave" coincided with Teddy

Roosevelt and his reformers taking over the city. Roosevelt, who was president of the New York City Police Board at the time, coined the phrase "muckrakers" to describe the sensational investigative reporting and talked Steffens and his fellow reporters into easing up on their "crime wave" stories.

There had been no increase in the crime rate at all, just more reporting of what had been going on for years. As soon as Steffens and his colleagues stopped reporting on the "crime wave," public agitation dissolved, the lock and guard-dog business fell off, and things were back to normal.

Competition among newspapers to be first with the news led editors to seek ever faster ways of getting the information. It used to take days, weeks, and sometimes months for most people to get the news, unlike today's instantaneous availability of what's happening. In the 1700s, a kind of "seeing-eye telegraphy" was developed, when messages were transmitted via a system of flags, poles, and lanterns located in strategic points along a route. The news could be sent much faster this way than via horse and rider. By the mid-1800s, France had five thousand kilometres of this visual telegraphy, and news could be sent from Paris to Calais in four minutes, according to technology author Wade Rowland. A British version of this system sent news between London and Portsmouth in fifteen minutes. A Canadian model in the late 1700s sent news and messages between Halifax and various points in Nova Scotia. In the mid-1800s, this visual telegraph system was overtaken by a technological breakthrough that brought people the news faster than ever before.

"What hath God wrought?"

Samuel Morse sent this message from Washington to

Baltimore in 1844 in a demonstration of his new device, the telegraph. What indeed! Not since Gutenberg's invention of the printing press four hundred years earlier would a new technology so revolutionize society. It was a long way from the time when Pheidippides ran from Marathon to Athens with news of victory over the Persians in 490 B.C. The telegraph defied time and space. It was a major milestone in the march from the news criers and balladeers, to newsletters and pigeons, to Pony Express and railways and ships in distributing the news. At the end of the 1700s, it took about forty-eight days for news to cross the Atlantic by sailing ship. By 1838, steamships had cut this down to as little as thirteen days. Reporters would sail out to the arriving ships and gather the latest European news by talking to passengers. Then they would summarize it and send it winging by pigeons to their various newspapers. Sometimes the reporters would row or sail ashore with the news and send their reports by horse. In 1833, the Pony Express used a relay team of twenty-four horses to take the news from New York to Washington in twenty hours. By 1847, the telegraph was replacing the pigeons and the horses, clattering the news in Morse Code to a dozen or more cities. Toronto and Hamilton were connected by telegraph in 1846, and shortly thereafter Toronto and Montreal were connected. The American Civil War of 1861–65 spurred the construction of a telegraph line across the United States.

The telegraph changed the very nature of news. Journalists turned their attention to reporting the latest happenings instead of featuring analysis and commentary as they had in the past. In 1894, a *London Times* correspondent was advised by his editor, "Telegrams are for facts; appreciation and political comment can come by post."

Until this time, serious news reportage had usually been

in the form of dawdling essays offering the writer's personal viewpoint of an issue or event, often with the "lead," the most important part of the story, buried deep in the article. The arrival of the telegraph caused a change in style to a terse lead at the beginning of the story – a quick, sharp, and clear first sentence – followed by paragraphs of diminishing importance that provided details on who, what, where, when, and why – the five Ws of journalism. This style of story was called the "inverted pyramid," which, says news historian Mitchell Stephens, "organizes stories not around ideas or chronologies, but around facts. It weighs and shuffles the various pieces of information, focussing with remarkable single-mindedness on their relative news values." This remains the dominant writing style of news reporting.

While most people hailed the technological triumph of the telegraph, some were not so sure. The American writer and philosopher Henry David Thoreau sneered, "We are eager to tunnel under the Atlantic and bring the Old World some weeks nearer to the New; but perchance the first news that will leak through into the broad flapping American ear will be that Princess Adelaide has the whooping cough." Indeed, the first news received by the British press via telegraph was the announcement from Windsor Castle of the birth of Queen Victoria's second son.

The *London Spectator* worried about the dangers of telegraphed news, saying, "The constant diffusion of statements in snippets, the constant excitements of feeling unjustified by facts, the constant formation of hasty or erroneous opinions must, in the end, one would think, deteriorate the intelligence of all to whom the telegraph appeals."

But most newspaper editors were unconcerned that speed

would breed superficiality; they wanted faster and ever faster news.

The completion of a transatlantic telegraph cable in 1866 and the growing web of telegraph lines around the world brought an end to the era of belated news. Only fifty years earlier it had taken four days for news of Napoleon's defeat at Waterloo to reach England. In 1821, it took two months for news of his death in St. Helena to be known in London. In 1789, it took several weeks before news of the French Revolution reached many rural villages in France. In his book *Public Opinion*, Walter Lippmann tells of an island where, in the early part of this century, a few French, British, and Germans lived quietly and happily together and where their only communication with the outside world was a ship bringing the mail once every month or two. In mid-September 1914, Lippmann says, the islanders met the boat and discovered that Britain and France had been at war with Germany since early August. "For six weeks, they had acted as if they were friends, when in fact they were enemies," Lippmann wrote. The telegraph and the telephone ended this kind of innocent isolation.

After Alexander Graham Bell invented it in 1876, the telephone, like the telegraph, became a key element in the fast collection and dissemination of news. The first known news report to be phoned in to a newspaper was an item on a lecture by Bell sent to the *Boston Globe* in 1877. Telegraph enthusiasts, however, initially dismissed the telephone as "a scientific toy," as the president of Western Electric called it. Another Western Electric senior executive declared, "This 'telephone' has too many shortcomings to be seriously considered as a means of communication." Even the chief engineer of the British post office in 1879 said there was little need for telephones because "we have a superabundance of messengers, errand boys. . . . If I want to send a message . . . I employ a boy to take it." Even some journalists disparaged the telephone on the grounds that it discouraged reportorial legwork.

When the telegraph arrived on the scene, it accelerated the development of news agencies, which provided news to many newspapers so that individual papers did not have to cover everything themselves. Three centuries earlier, the House of Fugger provided the roots of the first private news agencies. The Havas Agency, established in Paris in 1832, dispatched news by pigeons and semaphore to newspaper clients. A couple of decades before Havas, the British post office served as a government news agency, supplying foreign news to London papers twice a week.

In 1849, the Wolff Agency started in Berlin, and shortly after that Reuter began a news service in Germany and later in London, which focused on stock-market and business information. Both founders, Bernard Wolff and Paul Julius, Baron de Reuter, had been employed in Paris by Havas. Declaring his objective to be "first with the news," Reuter initially used hundreds of news-carrying pigeons, often attaching the same reports under the wings of three different pigeons to ensure the news would reach its destination. In the United States, an exchange of news among New York papers was established in the mid-1840s, beginning what would become the Associated Press (AP).

For more than a century, the news agencies were the world's most powerful news disseminators, until television news networks supplanted them at the end of the twentieth century. With their veneration for fact, agencies such as Reuters and

Associated Press were the world's most reliable source of what was happening. Its newsmen were everywhere. An Associated Press correspondent, Mark Kellogg, was with Custer at Little Bighorn; Frank le poer Power was with Gordon at Khartoum; and another AP correspondent witnessed the 1900 Boxer Rebellion in Beijing. Mahatma Gandhi once said, "I suppose when I go to the Hereafter and stand at the Golden Gate, the first person I shall meet will be a correspondent from the Associated Press."

In Canada, the Canadian Pacific Railway (CPR) had a monopoly on the distribution and sale of Associated Press reports. In 1907, the CPR doubled the price of providing AP news to three Winnipeg papers and they retaliated by starting a rival service using United Press and Hearst reports. Shortly afterwards, the CPR gave up its AP franchise and Canadian Press (CP) was formed to distribute AP – CP didn't start gathering news itself until 1917. At first, CP was given an annual federal government subsidy of $50,000 to lease telegraph lines, but it stopped taking the subsidy a few years later after much debate over the ethics of accepting government money.

The press agencies played a central role in the development of media independence. For much of the nineteenth century, both in Europe and North America, most newspapers were controlled by political parties, which, themselves, were developing into major organizations. The establishment of news agencies began to free newspapers from the parties. Because they provided news to papers of all political stripes, the wire-service reports had to be neutral. This soon brought most newspapers into a rough form of political balance and fairness.

Another key factor in bringing political independence to

newspapers was the arrival of advertising, which loosened the papers' reliance on the subsidy paid by a political party. The first newspaper advertising appeared in 1624 in the English newspaper *The Continuation of the Weekley Newes*, which offered a map of one of the battles reported in that issue. By the 1640s, papers were charging to publish appeals for the return of stolen horses, lost children, or lost articles. There were also advertisements for medicinal remedies, tea, beef, and fire extinguishers. Even Charles II in the late 1600s advertised in the newsbook *Mercurius Publicus* for the return of his lost dog, a spaniel with, the ad said, black and white streaks on its chest.

But advertising remained a marginal part of newspaper revenue for the next century or so. The first advertising in Canada appeared in the *Halifax Gazette* in 1752, which carried one for butter, one for a lawyer, and one for instruction in "Spelling, Reading and Writing."

An ad in the Montreal *Transcript* of the mid-1850s said, "Dr. Hoofland's Celebrated German Bitters" will cure "jaundice, dyspepsia, constipation, heartburn, heart fluctuations, dimness of vision, yellowing skin, heat flashes and constant imaginings of Evil and great Depression of Spirits." Another ad proclaimed the value of "Pink Pills for Pale People." There were ads for liquor, tobacco, and a multitude of patent medicines. The power of Holloway's Pills was exalted in the *New Brunswick Reporter* in 1846: "The mighty wonders of these extraordinary pills will do wonders in any of the following complaints. . . ." Then followed a list of thirty-six complaints, including "asthma," "fits," "piles," "worms of all kinds," "venereal infection and female irregularities."

It was not until the late 1800s that the new industries and large retail stores began advertising extensively, making ad revenue a major part of newspaper income. Without advertising, the average newspaper today would retail for $2.50 or more. Revenue from advertising reached its zenith in the spring of 1998 during the U.S. broadcast of the last episode of the TV series *Seinfeld*. A thirty-second spot during the show cost close to $2 million. The previous high had also been in 1998 during the broadcast of the Super Bowl, which cost advertisers $1.3 million for thirty seconds.

By the turn of the twentieth century, newspapers were reaching a far broader audience than ever before, now that most people in Europe and North America were able to read. This meant editors spent much of their time searching for exciting news that would keep the vast readership interested in buying papers. This search encouraged journalists to splash in the waves on top of the sea of public affairs rather than dive into the currents below the surface. It also led to the temptation for journalists to be entertainers rather than, as the eminent nineteenth-century U.S editor Horace Greeley described them a century and a half ago, "public teachers."

"It's entertainment they want!" said editor Noel Monks of Beaverbrook's *Daily Express* in London in the mid-1930s. And true enough, entertainment sells papers and boosts ratings in the twentieth-century print and electronic versions of Grub Street or the Yellow Press. The fear that "if you bore, you die" encourages editors to give entertainment values dominance. At the beginning of his career, Rupert Murdoch's appetite for sensationalism fanned sales of his newspapers in Australia and spurred his rise to global media power. In the 1960s, his papers rocked the country with sex exposés and brassy headlines such as in the *Sunday Mirror*: "Prowler Strips Woman Naked." Another read, "We Have Schoolgirl's Orgy

Diary." This was a style Murdoch perfected years later in England with his papers the *News of the World* and the *Sun*.

Although Canadian papers never became so salacious, they sought as much entertainment as possible, even from public figures. Former Ontario premier William Davis, who was nicknamed "Bland Bill" by the media, was once told by a Queen's Park correspondent for the *Globe and Mail*, "You're in the entertainment business. Do something that can excite us." It wasn't Davis's style.

This desire for excitement bothered Kent Cooper, the renowned general manager of Associated Press in the 1920s, '30s, and '40s. He once advised his reporters, "The journalist who deals in facts diligently developed and intelligently presented exalts his profession. . . . The reporter who resorts to the rouge pot to make his wares attractive convicts himself of laziness and ineptitude. . . . Artificiality and superficiality in news writing not only are unnecessary but ultimately must have a baleful influence on the reader."

Cooper's creed for AP was challenged, however, by journalists who felt that resorting to the "rouge pot" was necessary to excite the reader and expand circulation. Apart from reporting scandal and using sensationalism, one way newspapers excite readers is through social advice columns such as the one written by Ann Landers. She once told me that she had received ten thousand letters in response to a column she had just written. In his entire career, the famed American columnist Walter Lippmann never received that much response to anything he wrote. Miss Landers said the subject that elicited such widespread interest was whether, in installing a new roll of toilet paper, you should let the end come over the top or hang down the back. The public interest in that burning issue had demonstrated, Miss Landers told me, the power of the press. Her advice was to let the toilet paper come over the top.

During my years in Washington, I once filled in as a correspondent for the London *Daily Mirror,* one of the most successful of the Fleet Street tabloids. The pay was handsome, but the professional satisfaction was minimal. A major international story might merit three or four sentences, and sometimes my stories would be cut to one or two sentences. Most of the newspaper was devoted to advertising and "rouge pot" stories of crime and scurrility. What the *Mirror* really wanted from Washington was political scandal and back-corridor gossip. At the same time I was reporting for the *Mirror,* I was also a "stringer" correspondent for *O Estado* of São Paulo, Brazil, one of the world's great newspapers, comparable to the *London Times, New York Times,* or *Le Monde* in Paris. It had an insatiable appetite for nuanced and detailed stories of political events. It didn't hold a candle to the *Mirror* in circulation, nor did it pay as well, but its readers were far better informed and equipped to make judgements on the issues of the day, and for me it was far more professionally satisfying.

For much of the twentieth century, ballyhoo journalism has fuelled many North American papers, as shown by the "Front Page" antics in Chicago in the 1930s, the gaudy tabloids in New York, or the post-Second World War years of the *Toronto Star* (known then as "the last home of razzle-dazzle journalism"), the Toronto *Telegram,* or the *Vancouver Sun.* More recently, the *Sun* newspapers in Toronto, Ottawa, Edmonton, and Calgary adopted a remarkably financially rewarding and moderately cleaned-up version of the Grub Street approach to journalism. But nowhere is the intent to shock and amaze readers on every page more in evidence than in the tabloid press in London,

England, led by Rupert Murdoch's *Sun*. Whether covering the trial of O. J. Simpson, the life and death of Princess Diana, or the private affairs of Bill Clinton, not even the raciest American "tabs" could match the brazenness of the *Sun*.

Ballyhoo journalism has also crept into the news on radio and television, especially on commercial stations and networks. It was a subversion of the news that the founder of the CBC News Service in 1941, Dan McArthur, abhorred, warning his editors about "showmanship creeping into the news."

Throughout history, there has been this tug of war between news as entertainment and news as enlightenment. In Roman times, in the Middle Ages, in the Grub Street days, in the Roaring Twenties, and still today technology has played a central role in this battle. The inventions of Gutenberg, Morse, Bell, and others provided ways to spread and speed the news around the world to people who earlier had little knowledge of what was going on. We've gone from writing on clay tablets to printing on paper, and to sending words through cyberspace. Each of the developments of printing, telegraphy, broadcasting, and the Internet has fundamentally changed the form of gathering, editing, and transmitting the news, as well as affecting its substance. Today, the promised technology that will merge the telephone, television, radio, computer, and newspaper signals yet another enormous change in what kind of news we get and how we get it.

Along the way, in their search for bigger audiences, many news practitioners have used technology to turn the news business into show business. Back in the 1800s, Henry David Thoreau was sceptical about the impact of the new technology of journalism. "Our inventions are wont to be pretty toys which distract our attention from serious things," he wrote. "They are but improved means to an unimproved end."

It was the "end" that particularly worried Canadian writer and communications philosopher Harold Innis. He felt that the media, in the race for higher circulations, elevated instinct above intellect. "A prevailing interest in orgies and excitement was harnessed in the interest of trade. . . . The necessity for excitement and sensationalism has serious implications," he wrote.

Never before have those implications been more serious and more important than now, in the last days of the twentieth century.

4

The Three Walters

For me, the journalism of the twentieth century is personified by three Walters: one a solemn élitist; one a high-spirited gossip; and one a genial uncle. Walter Lippmann, Walter Winchell, and Walter Cronkite each had more influence on journalism than anyone else in this century, I believe, and together they personified the battle between news as entertainment and news as education.

In Canada, *Winnipeg Free Press* editor John Dafoe came close to rivalling Lippmann's influence among the powers-that-be of the first four decades of the century. In Britain, Geoffrey Dawson of the *Times* played a similar role. Winchell had no counterpart in Canada, with the possible exception of Gordon Sinclair, the cocky, opinionated, and immensely popular *Toronto Star* reporter and broadcaster. The 1971 Davey Report on Mass Media found Cronkite to be the most popular newsman in Canada. He was rivalled only by Norman DePoe, the CBC's legendary Ottawa correspondent in the 1950s and

'60s. DePoe, as one columnist wrote, had "the smell of news" about him.

The three Walters, who regularly wrote and talked to millions, made an indelible impression on their audiences, providing information and shaping attitudes as no one had before. Each of them reflected a competing style of journalism: Winchell was a gossip-monger; Lippmann was an opinionated columnist; and Cronkite was a factual reporter. They were phenomenally successful and became household names, but by the end of their careers, each one of them was disillusioned. Lippmann soured on the ability of the public and politicians to know enough detail to make intelligent judgements on public affairs. Winchell became bitter when he saw the public applause fade for his frenzied, bare-knuckle style of reporting. And Cronkite was dismayed by show-business values taking over television news at the end of the century.

"Facts are sacred," *Manchester Guardian* editor C. P. Scott declared. "Rigid factuality," demanded the founder of the CBC News Service, Dan McArthur, who considered news to be "a public trust." When he was asked to name the three most important qualities of reporting, American publisher Joseph Pulitzer replied, "Accuracy. Accuracy. And accuracy."

For his part, Walter Winchell was not someone who would ever allow accuracy to spoil a good story, and yet he was one of the century's most influential journalists. A second-rate vaudeville hoofer but a first-rate gossip columnist, Winchell was a Grade 4 drop-out who fancied himself a world-affairs thinker.

"Democracy is where everybody can kick everybody's ass," Winchell believed, and kick he did both in his columns and his

Sunday-night radio show, which he always began by saying, "Good evening, Mr. and Mrs. America and all the ships at sea! Let's go to press!" in a high-pitched, staccato delivery of, he claimed, 197 words a minute. His breezy mix of show business and politics was eagerly consumed by the biggest audience any journalist has ever had – at his height, 50 million people read his column or heard his radio show, two-thirds of the entire U.S. adult population at the time. His column, syndicated to more than two thousand newspapers, was sprinkled with such insights as "Franklin Delano Roosevelt's Maw is Okay, America!" or impudences such as "I do wish the various parties would stop submitting their ballyhooey to me. . . . I know too much about politics to care." To Winchell, any whisper was truth, although he often protected himself with so-called "blind" items such as "What married producer of three B'way musicals pays rent for a chorus girl in each?" In possibly the first newspaper reference to John F. Kennedy's romantic life, Winchell wrote, "One of ex-Ambassador Kennedy's eligible sons is the target of a Washington gal columnist's affections. So much so, she has consulted her barrister about divorcing her groom. Pa Kennedy no like." When he had to retract what he had written, he'd phrase it so that most readers would think it was just another news item: "Don't believe the talk that . . ." or "Gossip-mongers pulled a wrongo when they whispered . . ."

Winchell exploited the seemingly insatiable public appetite for diverting gossip and simple certainties to offset the gloomy reality of the Depression and the early days of the Second World War. Because of his influence on the public, politicians kowtowed to him. President Franklin Delano Roosevelt eagerly sought Winchell's support, frequently inviting him to the White House for consultations. Roosevelt even assigned a senior aide to regularly provide Winchell with inside information in exchange for his support for the president's policies. J. Edgar Hoover slipped FBI secrets to Winchell in exchange for romanticizing the G-men in his columns and newscasts. Even Eleanor Roosevelt cultivated his favour.

At Winchell's urging, government policies changed and laws were amended, careers were made and broken with a word from him – he had a long "drop dead" list of individuals he attacked. Murderers and racketeers surrendered to him instead of the police. He was a major force in persuading the American people to support war against Nazi Germany, and after the war, he was influential as a Cold War warrior, a hunter of reds and a supporter of the war in Vietnam.

Winchell did it all with breathless tension, a focus on celebrity, dollops of sensationalism, and a paucity of objective facts. It takes time to dig out the facts of important stories, and the idea of truth being the daughter of time escaped Winchell. "Christ, kid," he once told me during the 1960 Democratic Presidential Nominating Convention in Los Angeles, "if I took the time to check all the facts and rumours before writing them, I'd never have time at all to write or broadcast."

It was the only time I met the man whose radio program had so inspired me as a youngster selling newspapers on a Toronto street corner. In a way, he, too, had been a newsboy shouting "Extra . . . Read all about it!" only he'd done it on a world stage. Now, as we munched hot dogs and chatted in his cramped Mutual Broadcasting System convention studio next to the CBC booth, he was a shell of his former glory. In his heyday, he had swayed tens of millions, but the glamour was gone and the applause was fading. Wearing his trademark snap-brim fedora, which now hid a bald pate, in shirt sleeves and a loosened tie, he used arrogance to shield his dimming stardom. "Those bastards are all pygmies," he told me, looking out at the passing parade of politicians and journalists going in and out of the convention hall where John F. Kennedy was being nominated as the Democratic presidential candidate. "I could buy and sell any of those shits anytime. They all owe me. . . . You know, we're all in the gossip business. That's all that's going on here, just gossip, and everybody knows it."

My juvenile admiration for him crashed onto the paper-littered studio floor. I remember thinking, If gossip is all it is, then I'm in the wrong business.

Winchell's flash and vendettas were lapped up by millions, but they also earned him the contempt of many, including writer John Crosby, who called him "a cross between a weasel and a jackal," and actress Ethel Barrymore, who said, "I don't see why Walter Winchell is allowed to live." Nevertheless, Winchell changed the face of American journalism, and he remains a guiding spirit behind the push to turn the news business into show business.

If Walter Winchell was the quintessential journalist as gossip, Walter Lippmann was the epitome of journalist as teacher. Lippmann hated gossips passing as newsmen, calling them "Typhoid Marys." "They spread their infection without conscience," he said.

The eras of Winchell and Lippmann were roughly the same – from the Roaring Twenties to the war in Vietnam – but while Winchell's style was emotional and his power was in his influence on the masses in the streets, Lippmann's style was cold rationality and his power was in his influence on the decision-makers in the corridors of power. Journalism was a game for

Winchell, but for Lippmann it was a damn serious business. "The task of selecting and ordering the news," he once wrote, "is one of the truly sacred and priestly offices in a democracy."

As the high priest of serious journalism, Lippmann set out to educate and guide both the public and the policy-makers through the maze of national and international issues and events. He was born to the role, having wealthy parents, a Manhattan mansion, and travelling as a child to London, Paris, St. Petersburg, and Berlin. As a youngster he chatted with presidents William McKinley and Theodore Roosevelt, he studied philosophy at Harvard under George Santayana, and his schoolmates included T. S. Eliot and John Reed. He debated with George Bernard Shaw and H. G. Wells, and he did research for the great investigative journalist Lincoln Steffens. He was a friend of such judicial luminaries as Oliver Wendell Holmes, Learned Hand, and Felix Frankfurter. He advised Woodrow Wilson, helped devise propaganda for the United States during the First World War, and was a key adviser at the ensuing Versailles Treaty negotiations in Paris. All this before he was thirty.

Throughout his life, Lippmann knew everybody who was anybody. A note in his diary on a 1950 trip to Greece reads, "Saw the King, the Prime Minister, etc., the usual people." He knew every British prime minister and most French leaders, including Charles de Gaulle.

He began as a believer in the ideas of John Milton and John Stuart Mill that liberty depends on a totally free press and that if the public were given all the facts, it would be able to make the appropriate judgement. His propaganda work during the First World War, however, showed him how the public could be readily manipulated by lies and omissions. The supreme challenge for journalists, he believed, was to seek to keep pure the streams of fact that feed the rivers of opinion. He dismissed as dangerous entertainment the kind of journalism practised by Winchell, and he ridiculed almost everything on radio and TV news and in the mass-circulation tabloids of the time. Heaven knows how contemptuous he would be of what's seen today on most TV newscasts.

His firsthand knowledge of the ability of official propaganda to distort facts, to lie and "spin" the truth, and his sense of the increasing complexity and interaction of world events convinced Lippmann that it was impossible for the public to understand what was happening and make correct judgements. For most people, he said, the world had become "out of reach, out of touch and out of mind." He felt more comfortable with the élites who made those judgements, and for forty years his syndicated columns were aimed at the educated, informed, and powerful in and out of political office. His mission was enrichment and enlightenment; it certainly wasn't entertainment. "There can be no higher law in journalism than to tell the truth and shame the devil," he wrote in 1920.

Lippmann felt a key problem for the media was how to get people to make an "adjustment to reality." "The pictures inside people's heads do not automatically correspond with the world outside," he wrote. Like Plato, he condemned advocacy based on unsupported opinion instead of facts and truth. "We do not first see and then define. We define first and then see," he warned. In a less philosophical context, one of Canada's greatest Parliament Hill reporters, the CBC's Norman DePoe, once echoed that view when he told me, "What the public really wants in the news is a confirmation of their own biases." In other words, most people shape the pictures they see to fit their own attitudes.

In an elegant, subtle writing style, Lippmann devoted his

life to trying to get those pictures in people's heads adjusted to reality. That sometimes got him into trouble with those who insisted the facts were wrong and their biases right: Lyndon Johnson, for instance, whom Lippmann thought had the wrong picture about Vietnam in his head, or Richard Nixon, who, Lippmann said, had the wrong picture about Watergate. Convinced that Johnson was consumed with a "messianic megalomania," he wrote, "There is a growing belief that Johnson's America is no longer the historic America, that it is a bastard empire which relies on superior force to achieve its purposes and is no longer an example of the wisdom and humanity of a free society. . . . It is a feeling that the American promise has been betrayed and abandoned."

Johnson, a pork-barrel master, once told Idaho Senator Frank Church, who had voiced support for Lippmann's anti-Vietnam war position, "Frank, when you want another dam or post office in Idaho, why don't you ask Walter Lippmann." Lippmann could understand Johnson's pique, but he was astounded when delegates attacked him at the right-wing-dominated Republican Presidential Nominating Convention in 1964, which named Senator Barry Goldwater as its presidential candidate. "Down with Walter Lippmann!" they shouted *en masse.*

But because of the weight he carried among the élites of the nation, presidents listened carefully, however reluctantly, to Lippmann's words. He was increasingly dismayed by what he felt was the diminishing ability of leaders, let alone the masses, to understand and untangle the complexities of world affairs. "The world about which each man is supposed to have opinions has become so complicated as to defy his power of understanding," Lippmann said. He also had a doleful view of public-opinion surveys and the attention paid to them by leaders. He believed polls "enfeebled" government and were "a dangerous master of decisions." His depression was evident at a lunch given for him by a group of Washington correspondents that I attended. I remember him telling us in a discussion about the Vietnam War, "I hate old men who make wars for young men to fight. . . . Perhaps we are going into a minor Dark Age." He later mused negatively about the ability of the media to educate the public to the reality that the United States, while still the world's greatest power, was not "omniscient, omnicompetent, omnipotent . . . not the leader of mankind and not the policeman of the world."

About the same time that Walter Winchell's career was winding down, so, too, was Lippmann's. The two lions of twentieth-century journalism, who worked at opposite extremes of the profession, were saluted by writer Alexander Woollcott as personifying an era: "The age of the two Walters, Lippmann and Winchell." It had been their age, but another journalistic age was arriving as they were leaving – the age of the third Walter – Walter Cronkite.

He was not a vaudevillian journalist like Winchell, nor an élitist like Lippmann. Walter Cronkite was, as Canadians are so often labelled, "nice." He was also a hard-digging reporter who revered facts. As anchor for CBS TV News and trained in print and radio, Cronkite touched all forms of mass media and became the symbol of the new era of TV journalism. In Sweden, the name for a TV news anchor became "Kronkiter."

The first time I saw his name was in 1946 when I was working with British United Press in Toronto, and his byline clacked out on a BUP teletype over a story from Moscow where he was the United Press correspondent. Cronkite was then thirty-two years old and had been a UP war reporter. He had spurned Edward R. Murrow, who had wooed him for radio news, but eventually he succumbed to the blandishments of broadcasting, where he became the world's most famous newsman.

Where Winchell dealt in exciting speculation and Lippmann in sober evaluation, Cronkite provided "just the facts," as he once told me. A ferociously competitive newsman, "old iron pants," as he was known because of his long stints in the anchor chair on election nights, had insisted on the title managing editor of his CBS newscast. This gave him much more power in shaping his newscasts and in deciding what was to go into his program than he would have had as anchor alone. He played a key role in directing CBS coverage of the Watergate story and the downfall of Richard Nixon. After leaving his anchor chair, he grew to regret and resent a trend towards trivialization in the TV news.

In a conversation we had when he retired, Cronkite worried about what he called "the giggle factor" in the news. "Showmanship? We don't need it. It's no damn good," he told me. He assailed the print media, too, for "trivializing the news" with trashy features and abbreviated reports on serious stories. Looking to the future, Cronkite worried that the quality of TV network news would sink even further in a scramble of bottom-feeding journalism. "It is not too far a stretch to say that the public dependence on television for the bulk of its news endangers our democratic system," Cronkite wrote in his autobiography, *A Reporter's Life*. "The sheer volume of television news is ridiculously small. The number of words spoken in a half-hour broadcast barely equals the number of words on two-thirds of a newspaper page. . . . Hypercompression of facts, foreshortened arguments, the elimination of extenuating explanation . . . all distort to some degree the news available on television. . . . Sound-bite journalism simply isn't good enough."

Cronkite's chagrin at the trends in TV news is echoed by his one-time competitor, NBC News anchor Tom Brokaw, who, in a CBC interview, was particularly critical of local TV news. "They cover distractions," he said. "It's not about journalism. I defy you to find any station in the [United States] that regularly covers the institution of local government." Coverage of inconsequential news has begun to spread to the network newscasts themselves, and as former CBC correspondent and CBS's *60 Minutes* anchor Morley Safer says, "There is generally a lowering of standards with so much crap passing as information."

Cronkite agrees. In local news, he says, "You have to have action in the first twenty-five seconds, any old barn burning or truck jackknife will do. But the real action is in the political discourse that's going to determine how we're going to lead our lives in the future." That's not being covered, Cronkite warns, and his great fear is that smash-and-grab journalism will come to dominate local and national broadcast news and the front pages of the mainstream press, as well as supermarket tabloids.

"I don't envy those many serious broadcast journalists," Cronkite says. "The lack of respect in which they are held by their network managers is rubbed in their noses every day when the network-owned stations put the trashy, syndicated tabloid 'news' shows on in the preferred evening hours once occupied by genuine news programs." He adds, "Newspapers, under similar pressure of falling circulation, are also guilty today of trivializing the news."

Cronkite's apprehensions about the future of news are well founded, and, like him, I always have hated news programs being called "shows." To me, the newscast was always a "program." Calling the news a "show," as is done almost universally, encourages showbiz values in the news. I'm in the news business, not show business. So, too, were Walter Cronkite and Walter Lippmann. The other Walter – Walter Winchell – was not; he was a showman masquerading as a newsman. And the values of that other Walter now seem to be infecting the newsrooms of North America, more so in the United States than in Canada, but beginning here, as well, pushed by managements more interested in fat profits than quality journalism.

5

"Spinning" the News

Just as sensationalism leads to a dumbing down of the news, so, too, does official lying and its more polite contemporary euphemism, "spinning." "Spinning" is akin to what Sir Winston Churchill called "terminological inexactitudes." Whatever the term, the point is to mislead the public, something that has been practised by society's leaders for thousands of years. While journalism is often said to be the world's second oldest profession, that honour really belongs to officials who lie to the public.

"The rulers of the State . . . may be allowed to lie for the good of the State," Plato said in the *Republic*. The iconoclastic, deep-digging Washington journalist I. F. Stone once put it more brutally. "All governments are run by liars," he told me. Echoing that belief with a sigh of regret is one-time Conservative cabinet minister John Crosbie, who wrote in his autobiography, *No Holds Barred*, "A person cannot be truthful in politics. And that's a terrible thing." One politician who certainly knew that was Richard Nixon, who, drunk and boasting one night, told his friend and campaign colleague Leonard Garment, "You're never going to make it in politics, Len. You just don't know how to lie." In the end, and despite extensive practice in lying, Nixon didn't make it, either. His blatant efforts to mislead people over his role in the Watergate cover-up eventually turned off the public and encouraged people not only in the United States but in Canada and much of the rest of the world to doubt the word of all politicians. Respect for national institutions diminished throughout the West. Nixon's lies ultimately cheapened political dialogue and turned people away from participating in that dialogue. Watergate helped to subvert the healthy scepticism among many journalists into unhealthy cynicism and malign prejudgement.

The money and the effort expended by today's authorities to obfuscate the truth dwarfs anything that kings, emperors, and dictators of the past used to mislead what they hoped was a gullible public. One of the earliest "spinners" of the news was Julius Caesar, who used the *Roman Gazette* to dramatize his triumphs, minimize his defeats, and muzzle criticism. He shaped the reporting of issues and events to his advantage, knowing he had to have that support to survive politically.

"Nobody likes the man who brings bad news," Sophocles once said, a thought reflected in the Shakespearean drama *Cleopatra* when a messenger arrives with news that Marc Antony has married Octavia. Hearing the news, Cleopatra attacks the messenger, calling him "an infectious pestilence" and saying he should be "whipped by wire," "stewed in brine," "smart in lingering pickle," be scalped and finally killed. It's a sentiment many a politician today feels about reporters. "Though it be honest, it is never good to bring bad news," concludes Cleopatra. With added sarcasm, that poor opinion of reporters was echoed this century by Jody Powell, President Jimmy Carter's press secretary, who said that reporters were "like those who watch the battle from afar and when it's all over come down from the hills to shoot the wounded."

The Romans, however, had more control over the reporters of their age than did Carter and his successors, and so the early journalists shaped their reportage to suit their leaders. A newsletter under the control of Edward IV in the late 1400s vividly described a military triumph of the king over his enemies in these admiring terms: "The Kynge, full manly, set forth even upon them, enterd and wann the dyke, and hedge, upon them, into the cloose and with great violence, put them up towards the hyll. . . . Many of them were slayne and . . . many drownyd, many rann towards the towne, many to the churche, to the abby and else where, as they best myght." Pentagon publicists handing out disinformation on the "smart bombs" used in the Gulf War were clearly following an old tradition, as were officials who briefed reporters during the Vietnam and Falkland wars.

In the sixteenth century, Henry VIII used newsletters to put his own spin on his complicated marriage arrangements. His daughter, Queen Elizabeth, used newssheets to justify her arrest of the Duke of Norfolk for trying to put Mary Queen of Scots on the English throne.

France's King Charles VIII used newsletters in the late 1400s to seek support for his invasion of Italy and also to dismiss talk of his ill health. In 1493, within a month of returning from his discovery of America, newsletter accounts of Columbus's voyage were printed in Antwerp, Basel, Florence, Rome, and Spain, and Columbus himself was not averse to spinning the news by writing stories that boasted of his travels and asked for support for future trips. "I promise this," said Columbus in a sixteen-page article on his discovery of America, "that if I am supported by our most invincible sovereigns with a little of their help, as much gold can be supplied as they will need, indeed as much of spices, of slaves for the navy, as their Majesties will wish to demand." When William of Orange in 1688 landed in England to lead the "Glorious Revolution," he brought his own printing press with him, to be certain he received favourable news coverage.

In the early 1500s, King Ferdinand and Queen Isabella in Spain required all printing to be approved by church and state authorities. In Germany in 1521, the Edict of Worms declared that all printers must submit news stories to the authorities prior to publication. In France in the 1560s, printers caught trying to evade censorship were flogged and thrown into the Bastille, and in England a printer was put to death for printing criticism of the Queen's religious policies. In Italy in 1574, there was a crackdown on independent editors by Pope Pius V because, as a contemporary wrote, "They write things that did not sit well with him."

Despite the censorship and threats, more newspapers appeared, some of them clandestinely, as people sought to follow the news. As early as 1548, an English newsbook declared its aim was to meet "the thursty desyer that all our kynde hath to know."

By the 1600s, that "thursty desyer" and the mass communication made possible by Gutenberg's presses brought more daring journalism. In an English newsbook of about that time, the editor wrote, "I shall never admit for any affection towards countree or Kyn, to be so partial as will wittingly either bolster the falsehood or bery the truth. . . ." The same editor, however, saw nothing partial in condemning the Pope as "that hydeous monster, that venemous . . . antichrist."

In the 1640s, the *Mercurius Civicus* was subtitled "London's Intelligencer or Truth impartially related . . . to prevent misinformation." In 1647, the editors of the *London Post* described the difficulties of journalistic independence: "Whosoever undertakes to write weekly in this nature, undertakes to sayle down a narrow channel, where all along the shore on each side are Rocks and Cliffs that threaten him. He onely is the Happy Steersman that can keep his course in the middle of the channel . . ." The "middle of the channel" has been pursued regularly by editors from the 1640s to today. The first English-language daily newspaper began in 1702 with a pledge of "delivering Facts as they come related and without inclining to one Side or the other."

Although under the Stuarts there was a period of relative freedom for English newspapers, that was ending by the mid-1600s. After the Civil War in England, Oliver Cromwell gradually reimposed the press controls the Tudor monarchs had earlier enforced. One of Cromwell's official censors, Sir Roger L'Estrange, commented that a newspaper "makes the multitude too familiar with the actions and counsels of their superiors, too pragmatic and censorious, and gives them not only an itch, but a kind of colourable right and license to be meddling with the government."

Rebelling against censorship, the poet John Milton wrote in 1644 what has become the basic document for freedom of the press, "*Areopagitica* – for the liberty of unlicensed printing." Ever since, it has been used to justify journalistic independence. Truth is stronger than falsehood, he said, arguing for a free marketplace of ideas. Censorship, he said, is "the greatest discouragment and affront that can be offered to learning and to learned men. . . . Give me the liberty to know, to utter and to argue freely according to conscience, above all liberties." Milton felt if all ideas were freely published, the best ones would win the most public support. An editor's total freedom, he said, was the prerequisite for an effective democracy. Milton assumed that the citizen would read all available journalism, absorb all political points of view, sort out the good ideas from the bad, and come to his own conclusion. People would be freed "by reading all manner of tractates and hearing all manner of reason." Two centuries later, these views were endorsed by John Stuart Mill, who felt that even a wrong opinion should be published because it might contain a grain of truth that would help people find the whole truth. "Even at the canonization of a Saint, the church admits and listens patiently to a 'Devil's Advocate,'" Mill said.

The controls to which John Milton had objected were strengthened when Charles II was restored to the English throne and eliminated pro-Cromwell editors. As a warning to the rest to toe the royal line, one editor was hanged and, while he was still alive, his body cut down, mutilated, disemboweled, and, finally, decapitated.

In 1712, searching for more subtle ways of imposing restraint on the press, the British government imposed stamp taxes on newspapers with the objective of pushing the cheaper, more popular newspapers out of business and forcing others to raise their prices. At the same time, the government enforced strict limits on what newspapers could print about parliament. It had always been a hard and dangerous task for the early reporters. The first news of parliamentary activities was reported in 1641, a dry, straight reportage of speeches, but even this did not last long. In the 1770s when once again journalists were allowed to report on parliamentary debates, some were flung into jail for their reporting and none were permitted to take notes. Reporters were allowed only to watch and try to remember the debate as they wrote their stories. William "Memory" Woodfall was the hero of the press in the 1770s because his phenomenal memory enabled him to quote members of parliament almost verbatim. By the mid-1780s, however, reporters were allowed to take notes freely.

Most French papers in those days were even more tightly controlled by the government than their British counterparts. On threat of death, editors were ordered not to stir political passions, attack religion, or disturb the order and tranquillity of the population in these pre-French Revolution days. Nevertheless, underground papers circulated attacks on the government.

The most influential French weekly paper in the years before the revolution, the *Gazette de France*, was guided by Cardinal Armand Richelieu and was a tool of its royal masters. Its editor, Theophraste Renaudet, once asked rhetorically, "Was it for me to examine the acts of government?" On July 17, 1789, for example, the *Gazette* reported the news from various European capitals, on a fire in Paris, on the king being presented with a book, but there was no mention whatever of the storming of the Bastille three days earlier that began the French Revolution. The paper went out of business after the revolution. Freedom of the press was declared by the French Constituent Assembly and where there had been four officially authorized newspapers in Paris before the revolution, by 1790 there were 335. Press freedom was short-lived, however. The Paris Commune began to crack down on editors in 1792, returning France to the tight censorship of the pre-revolutionary days. In 1799, Napoleon ended press freedom, and the number of newspapers fell back to four. "If I loosened the reins on the press, I would not stay in power three months," he said.

In Germany at one point in the 1850s, during a government crackdown on the newspapers, so many editors were being thrown into jail that papers hired what were called "sitting editors" who sat in for the editor until he was let out of jail.

One of the master spinners of the news at the time was Germany's Otto von Bismarck, the "Iron Chancellor." An early sophisticate at managing the news, Bismarck bribed reporters, subsidized newspapers, and wrote articles and letters, sometimes under fake names. When he felt Empress Augusta was a threat, he secretly commissioned an article attacking her and then told journalists that he was "indignant" at what he labelled a "notorious article."

The danger of a free press to authoritarian governments was evident in the flames of the American Revolution, which were fanned, if not started, by the press, much as the media encouraged the collapse of communism in Eastern Europe a few centuries later. "There is nothing so fretting and vexatious, nothing so justly terrible to tyrants and their tools and abettors as a free press," said American revolutionary patriot Samuel Adams in 1768.

American newspapers took up a journalistic crusade against their colonial masters in London during the 1735 trial in New York of editor John Peter Zenger, charged with seditious libel for his attacks on the authoritarianism of the colonial government. His lawyer argued that Zenger had a right to defend the cause of liberty "both of exposing and opposing arbitrary power . . . by speaking and writing truth." He was found innocent, setting the stage for a more aggressive American press to provide the rhetorical gunpowder of revolution.

Fearing the power of the American press to stir revolutionary fervour, the British governor of Massachusetts, Francis Bernard, warned in 1768 that no "civilized Government upon Earth" could function while being watched by "Tavern Politicians and censured by News Paper Libellers." The press was certainly his nemesis: the Boston Tea Party of 1773 was planned in the home of the editor of the *Boston Gazette*. With the Revolution won, Americans made freedom of speech and the press the First Amendment to the Constitution.

After the Conquest in 1759, the colonial authorities in Canada also had trouble with the press, much of which demanded more freedom for the country. The papers were more moderate, however, than their American counterparts in their opposition to colonial authorities. Even so, their editorial agitation alarmed officials. "It is one of the miserable consequences of the abuse of liberty that a licentious press is permitted to poison the public mind with the most absurd and wicked misrepresentations," said John Beverley Robinson, the attorney general of Upper Canada in 1838. In part, Robinson was responding to the inflammatory rhetoric of the editor of the *Colonial Advocate*, the future rebel leader William Lyon Mackenzie, who had written, "Wherever the press is not free, the people are poor, abject, degraded slaves. . . . The press is the life, the safeguard, the very heart's blood of a free country, the test of its worth, its happiness, its civilization."

Some Canadian editors were flung into jail for "treason" and for "libelling" colonial authorities. In a landmark case on freedom of the press in 1835, the great Halifax editor Joseph Howe was charged with dissent and sedition, but, with distinct echoes of the Peter Zenger trial a century earlier, Howe pleaded with the jury to "leave an unshackled press as a legacy to your children." The jury did, acquitting Howe even though the judge had directed they find him guilty.

Howe and Mackenzie were among the giants of the early Canadian media, as were George Brown of the *Globe* in Toronto and Sir Hector-Louis Langevin in Quebec. Like the pre-revolutionary press in the United States, the reform press of Canada railed against the British colonial masters. "At this time in the history of the world," said educator George Monro Grant in 1828, "it was impossible to be an editor without being a politician also." Indeed, most Canadian newspapers of the era were subsidized by one political party or another. Openly biased reporting was common. "Downfall of the Upper Canadian Oligarchy!" shouted one headline in Mackenzie's paper, adding, "Complete Success of Liberal Sentiments Over Tory Avarice!!!"

Despite their efforts, government authorities failed, as they had earlier failed in the United States and Britain, to muzzle the Canadian press. At the end of the 1800s, historian and journalist Goldwin Smith wrote, "The power of journalism, great as it is, is still on the increase. The real debate has been transferred from assemblies, deliberative no longer, to the press."

But four or five decades later, that thesis was rejected by political leaders in Alberta and Quebec who tried to mute the media just as their colonial predecessors had tried to do before them. "I feel glad to believe there will be no newspapers in Heaven," Alberta Premier William "Bible Bill" Aberhart commented in 1937 before imposing a new law, An Act to Ensure the Publication of Accurate News and Information. It was a gag law that eventually was struck down by the Supreme Court of Canada and the Privy Council in London. That same year, Quebec Premier Maurice Duplessis similarly tried to gag the media with his Padlock Law, which entitled him to shut down any publication he deemed to be harbouring communist activity. This, too, however, was ruled unlawful by the Supreme Court. "Public opinion . . . demands the condition of a virtually unobstructed access to, and diffusion of, ideas," said Mr. Justice I. C. Rand.

"Out of my way, you drunken swabs!" shouted Lord Horatio Herbert Kitchener in 1898 as he waded through war correspondents anxious to question him about the fighting in the Sudan. Lord Kitchener had reporters arrested and expelled from war areas because he believed they were a nuisance and could undermine his authority with their reporting.

Although there were war reporters centuries before him, William Howard Russell of the *Times of London* is regarded as the father of modern war correspondents. "The miserable parent of a luckless tribe" was his description of himself. A stocky Irishman, Russell was there for the Charge of the Light Brigade in 1854, the Indian Mutiny of 1857–58, and he covered the U.S. Civil War, the Franco–Prussian War, and the Zulu wars of 1879. Defying official efforts to make him sugar-coat his commentaries, Russell's vivid reports gave a mass audience its first chance to read about the realities of war, the poor leadership of many generals, and the terrible suffering of the wounded. His coverage led, among other things, to Florence Nightingale's mission to Crimea.

For centuries, officials have sought to use reporters as extensions of the government, especially in wartime. The roots of war propaganda can be traced back twenty-four hundred years to Sun Tzu, author of *The Art of War*. Unlike Russell, most journalists were willing partners with official propagandists, knowing that nothing builds circulation faster than news of war. Reports of battle successes, real or otherwise, were detailed in the *Roman Gazette*, in newsletters and newsbooks, sung by news balladeers, and have been splashed across the front pages of newspapers for the past four hundred years. War jumped up circulations everywhere; the bloodier the news, the better the sales. One good example of misleading sensationalism is much of the coverage of the American Civil War. Faked horror stories abounded, such as reports of Northern soldiers' eyes being strung together by Southerners like beads on a necklace. Southern press stories spoke of the heads of Confederate dead being cut off and used as footballs by whisky-primed Northern soldiers. The public lapped it up. "Where there is no news, send rumors," editor Wilbur Storey of the *Chicago Times* told his correspondents.

With rumours, atrocity stories, and many a fake battle description, newspaper circulation soared, increasing as much as 500 per cent for stories of big battles. The New York *Herald* assigned sixty-three reporters to cover the war, and another paper had eighty war artists sending back gruesome pictures.

Philip Knightly, in his book on war correspondents, *The First Casualty*, has this to say about Civil War reporters: "They measured up poorly to the task . . . ignorant, dishonest and unethical. . . . Dispatches they wrote were frequently inaccurate, often invented, partisan and inflammatory . . . accuracy became a minor consideration."

Newspaper reports of the First World War were similarly sensational as the media spilled over with the propaganda pouring from the military and political leaders. Headlines detailed horror stories such as British and French soldiers' eyes being gouged out, children's candy being filled with gunpowder by the Germans, and German soldiers chopping off the hands of babies and the breasts of Belgian nuns, all invented by the British military and eagerly splashed across the front pages.

Nothing matched the efforts expended in lying propaganda, suppression of news, and spinning it than that exercised by officials during the First World War. "We identified ourselves absolutely with the armies in the field," said correspondent Sir Philip Gibbs. "Their task," editorialized the *Times of London* about its war reporters, "was to sustain the morale of the nation. . . . Defeats they minimized, excused or ignored."

"More deliberate lies were told," Philip Knightly has said about the news coverage of the First World War, "than in any period of history and the whole apparatus of the state went into action to suppress the truth." Trying to rationalize the suppression of news, the head British censor, the chief of the press bureau, once banned a Reuters story about a defeat by saying, "If Reuters published the news, it would be believed and the public is already discouraged enough."

During the Spanish Civil War of the mid-1930s, reports by Ernest Hemingway and other great correspondents were sometimes more vivid than accurate. "In Spain," said George Orwell, ". . . I saw newspaper reports which did not bear any relation to the facts."

The Second World War produced less media sensationalism, probably because the factual reporting was horrible enough. As Associated Press correspondent Robert St. John remarked after the war, "We were just leeches, reporters trying to suck headlines out of all this death and suffering."

Although less blatantly propagandist than their counterparts in the First World War, the Second World War correspondents also were often co-conspirators with the military in misleading the public and becoming an integral part of the propaganda machine. As Reuters war reporter and later Ottawa columnist Charles Lynch once told me, "It's humiliating to look back at what we wrote during the war. It was crap. We were a propaganda arm of our government. We were cheerleaders. It wasn't good journalism. It wasn't journalism at all."

A wartime CBC News guide to its editors warned, "When the news is particularly grave, care should be taken to handle it in a way that will not unnecessarily alarm or depress listeners. . . . If more cheerful or encouraging war news is available, use it in the next item."

The quality of Korean War reportage was much the same, and no wonder since most of the correspondents in Korea had covered the war against Germany and Japan. But later in Vietnam, there was a new generation of war reporters who were young, aggressive, sceptical, and, above all, convinced the government and military were lying.

Most journalists in Vietnam began routinely doubting the word of government authorities after they saw things with their own eyes that the military repeatedly denied. When I first got to Saigon to report on the war in late 1967, I was startled by the hoots of derisive laughter that greeted some of the comments of the senior American briefing officers. After going out into the field and seeing the battleground, I understood the journalists' guffaws because what I saw for myself was dramatically different from official claims. According to the military, defeats were victories, lost villages were called "contested," American casualties were always "light" while the communist casualties "heavy," and intensive bombing was euphemistically called "accelerated pacification." In the macho military language of what was known as Pentagon East, a phrase we reporters repeatedly heard to describe U.S. tactics was "You grab them by the balls, and their hearts and minds will follow!" One bitterly contested fire fight I witnessed on a hill not far from Saigon in which I saw several U.S. Marines killed and others wounded was called a couple of days later by the briefing officer in Saigon "A minor skirmish with no injuries." No wonder the daily U.S. military briefing in Saigon was labelled "The Five O'Clock Follies." One senior officer, who supported the war despite his apprehensions about U.S. strategy, told me over a drink at the Continental Palace Hotel, "To quote Arthur Koestler [in *The Yogi and the Commissar*], 'In this war, we are fighting a total lie in the name of a half truth.'"

For the most part, the Vietnam War reporters followed the creed of Reuters, which noted in its style guide for its correspondents, "Reuters does not comment on the merit of events. . . . One man's terrorist is another man's freedom fighter."

Despite glowing statements from the military in Saigon and the Pentagon, the facts of the Vietnam War wounded and sometimes destroyed the official line. Peter Arnett, who covered the war for AP and the Gulf War for CNN, said that in his reporting he dealt with facts, not judgements. "We were witnesses, and like witnesses to robbery, accident, or murder, surely it was not for us to be judge and jury," he said.

Government officials had a different idea, however. "Don't forget which side you're on" was the message we correspondents got from the military and from authorities in Washington who were alarmed by factual, realistic reporting by war correspondents. They believed, correctly as it turned out, that once viewers saw dead American soldiers on their television screens, public support for the war would dwindle. I was startled during the Kennedy presidency when an old colleague of mine, Arthur Sylvester, became assistant secretary of Defense and told us the government not only had a right to lie, but that reporters had an obligation to go along with the lies. Journalists, he told us in a briefing at the Pentagon, have a "patriotic duty to disseminate only information that made the United States look good." He was admonished by Kennedy, but his theme was certainly echoed by Secretary of State Dean Rusk and many other high officials, especially later during the Johnson and Nixon presidencies.

The American military felt burned by the media coverage of Vietnam, believing it was the major factor in weakening public support for the war. It resolved never to let that happen again and so it rigidly controlled journalists' access to the American invasions of Grenada in 1983, Panama in 1989, and in the Gulf War of 1990. No Iraqi civilians were killed in the American bombings during the Gulf War, the Pentagon seemed to suggest, although officials admitted there was "collateral damage," which, in truth, meant dead Iraqi civilians but sounded like there weren't any. It tried to make the war look like a kind of video game, showing the pinpoint accuracy of missiles going through Iraqi military doors and down chimneys, even though it was subsequently discovered the bombs were much less precise than advertised. Sadly, the Pentagon's manipulation and mutilation of reality worked with the public. Surveys showed most Americans supported the Pentagon's censorship, and public support of the Gulf War rose to 85 per cent.

It was British Prime Minister Margaret Thatcher who taught the Americans how to tame the media and force them to follow the government line with the leash she put on the media in the 1982 Falklands War with Argentina. Correspondents were simply kept away from the action and fed nothing but government propaganda.

The official argument for withholding information or even for misleading reporters is to protect lives. In any fighting I've covered, however, the restrictions on media coverage were primarily designed to protect political reputations, not military lives. Besides, I know of no journalist who would knowingly endanger lives by his or her reporting.

One-time CBC correspondent Morley Safer, who became a big-time CBS correspondent, was once singled out by President Lyndon Johnson for not being "on the team." Johnson labelled Safer's reporting of the Vietnam War as "communist." When the president was repeatedly assured by his aides that Safer was a Canadian, not a communist, Johnson responded that well, anyway, he knew something was wrong with "the son of a bitch!" Johnson's fury at Safer and other correspondents in Vietnam is shown in a phone call he made to CBS president Frank Stanton. "Frank," he said, "are you trying to fuck me? Frank, this is your president and yesterday your boys shat on the American flag!" Clearly, Johnson did not want to hear, nor to have the American public hear, the facts as reported by Safer and others because they wounded Johnson's own theories. In the end, when reality caught up with presidential perception, Johnson was driven from office. It was a classic example of what British philosopher Herbert Spencer called the tragedy of the Murder of a Beautiful Theory by a Gang of Brutal Facts.

Recognizing the power of the media, politicians throughout the last couple of centuries have complained about not getting what they felt was fair coverage. President Johnson repeatedly called reporters and editors at the networks and major newspapers to complain. British and Canadian leaders made similar if less sulphurous calls.

Canadian governments have been more subtle than others in retaliating against what they perceive as their journalistic enemies. Prime Minister John Diefenbaker tried in the late 1950s to diminish the impact of the CBC's journalism, which he felt was undermining his government. Slightly more than two decades after the CBC was formed, a vengeful Diefenbaker took away from the CBC its power to regulate all broadcasting, and elevated private stations to equal status with the CBC, destroying the model of a public broadcasting system that prime ministers R. B. Bennett in 1932 and Mackenzie King in 1936 had set up.

About twenty-five years after Diefenbaker's actions, another Conservative prime minister, Brian Mulroney, outraged by what he felt was unfair treatment by CBC journalists and battered by pressure from the right wing of his party, slashed CBC budgets and tried, unsuccessfully, to force out the CBC president, Pierre Juneau.

One Sunday night when I was anchoring the CBC national news, we reported on a Montreal meeting addressed by Brian Mulroney, who, at the time, was making his run to dethrone Joe Clark as Conservative leader. As soon as the newscast was over, Mulroney was on the phone complaining to me: "The meeting was much bigger than your man said, and God, you mentioned hardly any of the big names there, people who are really influential and count. And it's not the first time I've been short-changed by you guys. I'm bloody mad about it!" A few weeks later, he called me again to complain. "I'm mad as hell," he said. "It's just not fair. You guys are not giving me a fair shake." When I got home that night after midnight, he phoned again, saying, "I'm still mad and the more I think about it, the madder I get. Here, let me put Mila on and she'll tell you how angry I am." On came the soft-voiced Mila, who earnestly said, "Yes, Knowlton, he really is angry." Not all leaders are that persistent in their complaints, but they all are sensitive to how the media portrays them because they know their future depends on it.

Damaging budget-cutting at the CBC reached its height, however, under Liberal Prime Minister Jean Chrétien, whose personal antipathy to CBC news coverage of himself was even more intense than Mulroney's and whose cuts significantly hurt the breadth and depth of CBC news activities. Chrétien carried scars from run-ins with the CBC French network, which he felt continually undermined him. He had long-held resentments at what he believed was the French network's scorn of him, particularly during the 1980 Quebec Referendum coverage. More recently, he was irked at an English-network public-forum program where he had seemed ill-prepared for the questions and felt he'd been set up.

French President Georges Pompidou had more success than Mulroney or Chrétien in getting the news to reflect his perceptions. During his presidency, the French TV network ORTF was a national government network, and if you worked for it, he declared, you "must always keep in mind that you are not talking for yourself, you are the voice of your country and your government." Lyndon Johnson, Brian Mulroney, and Jean Chrétien would have approved. Similarly, British prime ministers such as Winston Churchill, Anthony Eden, and Harold Wilson, bruised in the constant war between Fleet Street and Downing Street, tried to control the reporting of the BBC. At one point, when Churchill was a cabinet minister during Britain's paralysing General Strike in 1926, he even tried to take over the BBC and run it himself. Although while he was out of office in the 1930s Churchill thrived from his talks on BBC Radio, once in office he thought radio should be an instrument of the government. He also believed television was an utterly improper medium for news and political debate. He was suspicious of the media and thought that the BBC was "honeycombed with socialists – probably with communists."

In its early years, the BBC was forbidden by the government to cover elections or broadcast anything "controversial" and later was barred from reporting on upcoming issues that were to be dealt with in parliament. Hitler's Germany and Stalin's Russia used more brutal forms of media muzzling. In Russia, ownership of radios was severely restricted and listening to foreign newscasts was a serious offence. In Nazi Germany, you got five years in prison if caught listening to foreign radio stations.

The media, in pursuit of objectivity, sometimes were trapped into becoming an instrument for the most outlandish lies. A classic example is the media's coverage of Senator Joseph McCarthy's "red hunt," which tarred a generation of Americans in the 1950s. The media dutifully reported the senator's wildly inventive and profoundly inaccurate accusations about communist spies in government but, at first, provided no context and failed to note his many inconsistencies and contradictions. As a correspondent in Washington during those days, I shared with most of my colleagues an excessively rigid commitment to objectivity, reporting what was said but shying away, initially at least, from providing the background and context because we feared doing so would be labelled editorializing. It was frustrating to know we were being used by McCarthy, but most of us felt we should not do anything about it. In time, however, the media began showing a fuller portrait of McCarthy that demonstrated the recklessness of his accusations. It was not enough to quote neutrally his every lie and libel, for the truth took years to catch up. As Mark Twain once noted, "A lie can travel half way around the world while truth is still putting on its shoes."

In Canada, politicians, including prime ministers, also use "terminological inexactitudes" and "enriched" descriptions of reality, if not to the same extent as their American counterparts. Just listen to them during an election campaign. They prefer to put the emphasis on image than on the discussion of issues, which is why they increasingly seek to appear on TV and radio talk shows, where they can more readily avoid tough questions from knowledgeable journalists. Even comedy programs, such as *The Royal Canadian Air Farce* and *This Hour Has 22 Minutes*, feature political leaders from time to time, where they display their sense of humour, if not their policy objectives. No wonder Canadian humorist Stephen Leacock once said, "It's simply in the nature of a politician to promise a bridge in one election and a river to run under it in the next." Even Canada's one-time symbol of integrity, the RCMP, has been caught playing fast and loose with the truth – over its burning of barns in Quebec in the early 1970s, for instance – as has the Canadian military over its actions in Somalia in the 1990s.

Prime Minister John Diefenbaker had a particular preference for assertion over evidence in trying to heighten his prestige. I covered him at the United Nations on one occasion at which he made a strong anti-communist speech to the General Assembly. Two weeks earlier, Soviet Premier Nikita Khrushchev had been at the UN, where he demonstrated his distress with the West by banging his shoe on his desk. In Mr. Diefenbaker's mind, however, the two occasions merged. A couple of years later, I followed him in a federal election campaign and repeatedly heard him say that he had spoken out so strongly against communism that Mr. Khrushchev had taken off his shoe and banged it on the table. He always got a huge round of applause for having elicited this response from Khrushchev, and after a while I think he began to believe it himself. Any effort on my part to note in my reportage that the UN records showed Mr. Diefenbaker had spoken two weeks after the incident brought scorn from the prime minister and no change in his assertions.

In the Gulf War, deposed Kuwaiti leaders hired an American public-relations company to manage their images. The company came up with the testimony of a fifteen-year-old Kuwaiti girl, who told a U.S. congressional group she had seen Iraqi soldiers yanking babies out of a hospital and leaving them to die. It was powerful, persuasive stuff, but, as was later discovered by investigating journalists, it was a total fabrication. The girl herself turned out to be the daughter of the Kuwaiti ambassador to the United States and Canada.

Is it, in the end, a good thing for government leaders to lie in what they think are the best interests of the country, as Plato claimed? Surely not. Still, the practice is not going to stop, for we seem to live in an era of pretence, and political leaders think that they must, at times, lie. But there is a price to be paid. When lies and artifice are uncovered, as they usually are by the media, the inevitable result is public disillusion with a political system that encourages lying and with those who do the lying.

Government falsifying also encourages private falsifying. Corporations put a gloss on dross or obfuscate reality in an effort to enhance their images or sell products. Corporate press releases often get used in full by the media because editors have space to fill and have decreasing resources to do their own reports. This has led the media to rely on free but tainted public-relations material aimed primarily at serving not the public but the corporation. It has been estimated that half of all the news we get in the mainstream daily media comes from public-relations officials. Ray Argyle, president of Argyle Communications, one of Canada's most successful PR organizations, suggests it runs as high as 80 per cent.

Just like politicians, corporate executives want reporting to be shaped to fit their objectives; they want a sympathetic, if not sycophantic, news media, not one that's assertively independent. Sympathy and sycophancy are not in the news media's job specs, however, for the journalist's role is to come as close as possible to providing a fair reflection of reality.

Even union leaders sometimes want the media to dance to their tune, as in 1996 when the *Toronto Sun* was bought by its own management, backed, in part, by a loan from the Ontario Teachers' Pension Fund. Leaders of the Ontario Teachers' Federation demanded that the *Sun* be more pro-union in its journalism and less supportive of government cut-backs in return for their pension fund's $70-million investment. While grateful for the investment, the *Sun* refused to change its spots. Its editor-in-chief, Peter O'Sullivan, said, "I'm sure they're smart enough to know that the opinions of this newspaper are not for sale." The *Sun* kept the money and its opinions.

In the United States in recent years, mega-corporations have been taking over networks and have been examining newsroom practices and standards in regard to their business efficacy. Since their overriding objective is a fatter bottom line, the danger is that the new owners will frown on controversial reportage, especially if it intrudes on one of their own products or services. How investigative will General Electric-owned

NBC be of a suspect product produced by GE? Or how is CBS news coverage affected when Michael Jordan, the chairman of CBS's owner, Westinghouse Electric, goes to Beijing and publicly promises the Chinese that his company will support efforts to abolish the sanctions against China's buying nuclear technology? How tough were the Thomson papers in covering news of the Hudson's Bay Co. when Thomson owned it? When newspaper and broadcasting ownership shares lie in a corporate safe next to ownership shares in other companies, judgements are bound to be coloured to reflect a common corporate good. It may make business sense to pull your editorial punches, but it violates every bone in a journalist's body.

Those in authority, whether in government or in the private sector, must be able to cope with a prying media, a sometimes obstinate, cantankerous, and occasionally even disrespectful media, if the right of people to know what is really going on in the world is to be preserved. Part of the media's job is to enlarge public understanding of uncomfortable problems, even though it inevitably distresses some people. Oliver Wendell Holmes put it succinctly: "There must be freedom for the thought you hate." Without that freedom, you don't have a democracy.

The role of the media as a lie detector is crucial. Echoing Holmes, Walter Lippmann once noted, "There can be no liberty for a community which lacks the means by which to detect lies." "The means" are a strong media spurred by their responsibility to society, not a dumbed-down media weakened by official lies, spinning, and junkyard news.

6

Drops of Ink

A small drop of ink . . .
makes thousands, perhaps millions, think.

For years, that poetic salute to newspapers penned by Lord Byron adorned the fireplace in the parliamentary press gallery lounge in Ottawa. It was placed there in 1920 by the illustrious editor of the *Ottawa Citizen*, Charles Bowman, and reminded journalists that for hundreds of years, drops of ink carried the news.

But for how much longer? Since the 1970s, more people have been getting their news from television than from the presses of the post-Gutenberg era. And now within a generation the Internet may well become our principal source of news.

"The last of the smoke stack industries" is the way futurist Alvin Toffler described daily newspapers in his forecast of a "demassified media" – the collapse of mass media into the specialization of micro media, as has occurred already with magazines and radio, and is now happening with television.

In 1997 and early 1998, newspaper profits in the Western world have been skyrocketing, and there has been much self-congratulatory back-patting among publishers and editors. Their large profits, however, came more from low newsprint prices and burgeoning economies than from much-trumpeted newspaper facelifts. A jump in the price of newsprint or a pause in economic growth would quickly silence the publishers' hosannas.

Every industry goes through the stages of impetuous childhood, sober maturity, and artery-clogged old age. While there are exceptions, most newspapers are reaching the final stage, responding to the onslaught of television and the Internet by reeling about in gaudy headlines and layouts, celebrity news, colour, graphics, how-to features, contests, and advice to the lovelorn, all wrapped up in fast-food journalism. But these flashy changes are just playing at the margins of the issue, like offering "new and improved" laundry detergent. In going down market, newspapers are ignoring the fundamental reality that their strength lies in offering intellectual meaning rather than emotional experience. Television does the latter far better. Newspapers are left brain, TV is right brain, while the Internet – with its mix of audio, video, and text – is rapidly becoming simultaneously both a right- and left-brain medium.

Within a couple of decades, the newspaper industry may well no longer be a news*paper* industry; at best, those papers with a reverence for quality news and which are sufficiently far-sighted will become information companies, supplying news to a variety of delivery systems, especially the Internet. "I just can't picture papers surviving without going electronic with much of their product in ten or twenty years," says Lib Gibson, general manager of the Globe and Mail Information Services. "I just can't imagine it." Increasingly troubling questions for newspapers, according to the industry magazine *Editor and Publisher*, include: "Are newspapers really doing enough to meet the new sorts of threats coming at them from cyberspace? And by the time these publishers finally do wake up to the new reality, will it be too late?"

Newspapers that survive will go through what American media analyst Roger Fidler, formerly of the Knight-Ridder papers and now a professor at Kent State University in Ohio, calls a "mediamorphosis," a creative transformation into a new electronic medium. For newspapers to survive Toffler's "demassification," they must go through Fidler's "mediamorphosis."

But for all the exciting, pioneering prospects of the new media, I find it heartbreaking to contemplate the uncertain future of many paper and ink newspapers. They are a romantic old flame who has a deeper hold on my affections than the new svelte hussy on the block, the Internet, will ever have. The bloodless medium of binary numbers, pixels, fibre optics, megabytes, hypertextuality, and digitalization pales by comparison. As I write these words, memories of half a century ago come swirling back, and I can again see and hear and feel the tremendous roar and power of the presses rolling out hundreds of thousands of newspapers. I can smell the deep, sweet, almost cloying aroma of the ink. It was an overpowering thrill to witness the ear-splitting mating of machinery and creativity, whether the Maclean Hunter presses were printing a weekly paper for Ontario high schools that I once edited or churning out a weekly neighbourhood newspaper I later edited in Toronto. I loved watching, awestruck and slightly frightened, the thunderous presses of the daily newspapers in Toronto, Vancouver, and Halifax. I loved, too, the clacking of the long-gone linotype machines, with their gangly steel arms reaching out to grasp the metal type.

The old-time newsrooms themselves, for a naïve, eager young journalist, were like a carnival world of people laughing, shouting, banging away at typewriters, sipping booze (sometimes coffee) out of paper cups, and munching sandwiches as agency teletypes throbbed with news from Paris or Moscow or London and bells rang for important stories. That garish wonderland – its floor littered with paper and, above all, its air clouded with cigarette smoke – is gone now. Most newsrooms have become as prissy as insurance company offices. There's no smoking, no bells ringing, no shouting; editors and reporters quietly peer at their computers. In some newsrooms, there are even rugs on the floor.

Print in one form or another – those drops of ink Lord Byron wrote about – has been the principal conveyor of news since the days of Julius Caesar. In the 1600s, as newsletters and newsbooks gave way to newspapers, the constantly improving technology of printing gave newspapers overwhelming dominance in the dissemination of the news, and until the late twentieth century, newspapers were the most powerful instrument of conveying information the world had ever known. Publishers and editors such as Northcliffe, Beaverbrook, Hearst, Pulitzer, and, in Canada, Brown, Atkinson, Dafoe, Bowman, the Siftons, and the Southams had influence and power envied by emperors, presidents, and prime ministers. Because newspapers were their avenue to the public, politicians feared, loathed, and respected the power of the press. They sought to manipulate publishers and editors through bribes, threats, and giving insider access. They knew that to be a leader, they had to have newspaper support.

The first tremors to shake this mountain of newspaper power came from radio, which, initially, newspapers thought was more a toy than a threat. London *Daily Mail* magnate Lord Northcliffe sponsored a blockbuster radio concert to introduce radio to the British in 1920, as did *Toronto Star* publisher Joe Atkinson two years later for Torontonians. In the early years of radio in Canada, newspapers ran stations in Toronto, Winnipeg, Vancouver, Halifax, Montreal, Calgary, Edmonton, Regina, London, Hamilton, and Quebec City. It was a similar story in the United States, where one of the first significant newscasts was on KDKA Pittsburgh, which broadcast the 1920 presidential election results from the newsroom of the *Pittsburgh Post*.

Most publishers thought radio was an entertainment medium and useful only for its promotional value for their papers. It would, as Canadian Press said at the time, "whet the public appetite [for news] rather than satiate it." But, within a few years, most newspapers had retreated from dabbling in radio, leaving the medium in Canada and the United States to hustling entrepreneurs who converted the airwaves into a cornucopia of advertising profits. In Britain, the emergence of the commercial-free BBC spared newspapers the confrontation with radio over advertising.

Publishers and editors carped from the sidelines that radio threatened their own advertising revenue. In the 1930s, the number of commercials carried by the Canadian Radio Broadcasting Commission (CRBC) and, later, by the CBC so alarmed the newspapers that they protested vigorously to the government. The *Financial Post* accused the CBC of endangering Canada by weakening newspapers through diversion of advertising money. The newspapers, the *Post* thundered, "are the bulwarks of national unity in this country."

In the early days of radio, newspapers also saw chinks being opened in their exclusive coverage of news events – the source of their power. "If news is known by the public through radio broadcasts," said *Editor and Publisher* in 1927, "there is no logical incentive to buy a newspaper to get the news." For major events, radio did original on-the-spot reporting, and listeners eagerly followed the broadcast reports, absorbed by radio's emotionalism and immediacy. Radio also had the advantage of always being first with breaking news, since broadcasting basically had no deadlines. Newspapers began to stop publishing Extras.

Being forced to accept radio into the journalistic club for big events was bad enough, but newspapers were also bitter at radio for reporting news on the cheap simply by scalping the everyday news the papers carried and airing it as their own. "News robbery!" declared Canadian Press general manager J. F. B. Livesay. The editor of the *Calgary Herald*, J. H. Woods, protested against any news at all being carried by radio. "Newspapermen spend years in learning how to handle news with moderation and with accuracy," he said. "It is not a job that can be trusted to anyone who speaks into a microphone."

As radio became more powerful, many observers predicted it would be the death of newspapers, stealing their advertising and turning their readers into listeners. News began to thrive on radio, and Walter Winchell, Edward Murrow, Gordon Sinclair, Lorne Greene, and Matthew Halton all became household names. But there was a big enough pie for all and newspapers still made record profits. They would have made even more without radio, of course, but Canadian and American papers continued to do very well indeed.

Since their fears of radio's impact had not been realized, newspapers initially felt that television would merely be another pesky rival, not a killer. Their complacency can be seen in comments in the *New York Times* review of the TV display at the New York World's Fair in 1939. "The problem with television," the *Times* concluded, "is that the people must sit and keep their eyes glued on a screen; the average American family hasn't the time for it."

But the average American family made the time for it, and today over 3 billion people around the world spend about half of all their leisure time staring at that box of wires, tubes, and circuit boards. In Canada, the average viewer spends twenty-two to twenty-three hours a week in front of the television set.

At the beginning of television, newspapers sniffed haughtily at the thought of the new medium providing any serious competition for the news audience. Most broadcasters also thought that TV didn't have any significant role to play in disseminating the news: the CBC didn't even have a newscast when television began. Television was for entertainment, not news, the CBC said.

The newspaper owners sat contentedly back and watched what global news magnate Rupert Murdoch has called the "rivers of gold" – revenue from circulation and advertising – continue to pour in, seemingly unaffected by television. "Owning a newspaper . . . can be almost twice as profitable as owning a paper box factory or a department store," said the 1971 Davey Report on Mass Media. A few years later, the Kent Commission on Newspapers reported that the return on net assets for Canadian newspapers averaged 33.4 per cent from 1974 to 1980. In the United States, average operating profits for newspapers peaked in 1987 at 24.1 per cent.

But television news got better and more aggressive, quickly becoming both a journalistic and an economic threat to newspapers. In the early 1950s, the average American adult watched

TV news for about fifteen minutes a week. By the early 1970s, it was 128 minutes, and 330 minutes by the mid-1990s, according to the Pew Research Center. As the 1970s rolled on, TV news began to dominate, and by mid-decade most people were primarily depending on television for their news, whether it was CBS's *Evening News*, the CBC's *The National*, or the BBC's nine o'clock news.

Around the world, newspaper circulation has been falling ever since television news moved into the driver's seat. In the period 1992–96 in Sweden, it was down 12 per cent; in the Czech Republic, down 36 per cent; in Hungary, down 17 per cent; in the United Kingdom, down 5 per cent; and in Italy, down 6.5 per cent. During those five years, newspaper circulation in the European Community fell by 4.2 per cent – 3.5 million fewer daily newspaper buyers. In the United States, total circulation fell from around 61 million in 1992 to around 58 million four years later. Some forecasters predict it will fall even faster in the years ahead, while others project that the decline will level off. In Canada in 1996, the circulation of our 105 daily newspapers averaged 5.2 million copies a day, down 100,000 from the previous year, and in 1997 it was just above 5 million. From 1980, Canadian daily circulation fell nearly 800,000, although with Conrad Black's new national paper some of that drop may be erased in the immediate future.

In the 1960s, about 75 per cent of Americans read a paper every day. Now only 40 per cent do, according to the *Los Angeles Times Mirror*. The figures are higher for Canada, with about 62 per cent of Canadians reading a paper every day, compared with 80 per cent thirty years ago. Particularly worrisome for newspapers is the dramatic drop in young readers. In 1970 in the United States, 76 per cent of people under thirty-five regularly read newspapers. It's now around 20 per cent. Those in their twenties and younger largely don't read the papers at all, and according to the Newspaper Association of America, even adult readership has fallen from about 80 per cent in 1970 to about 59 per cent today. Failure to reach the younger generation is also seen as a problem in Britain. "If we fail to make contact with that group, then we're done for," warns David Bell, chairman of the *Financial Times of London*.

A survey by Intel Corp. asked a group of people born after 1971 where they think they'll turn for news in ten years time. About 60 per cent said the Internet; 31 per cent said broadcasting; fewer than 10 per cent said the print media. A survey by MSNBC showed 65 per cent of its viewers feel that by the year 2000 they expect to get all their news from the Internet. A United Press International survey in mid-1998 showed 80 per cent of computer users believe the Internet will eclipse print newspapers as a major source of news and information within five years. A mid-1998 survey by the Pew Research Center showed 20 per cent of American adults, or 36 million people, get news from the Internet at least once a week. That compares with 6 per cent and 11 million two years ago. Among the eighteen to twenty-nine age group, 30 per cent go to the Internet at least once a week for their news.

While the young are particularly inclined to go electronic for their news, the population as a whole has been shifting from print to TV. In 1997, a *Time*–CNN poll showed 59 per cent of Americans depended on TV for news and 23 per cent on newspapers. Even more alarming for newspapers is a study by Media Dynamics, Inc. that shows that of the time spent with the media

(TV, radio, newspapers, and magazines), Americans spend about 52 per cent of that time with TV and only 7 per cent with newspapers.

The same pattern likely will happen in the twenty-first century, as families shift from newspapers and television to the Internet. The users of Internet news services are already reading newspapers less and watching television less. Among users of the PointCast news service, 46 per cent said that they're now spending less time reading newspapers and 21 per cent said they're watching less TV. The *Economist* says that those who are on-line are watching about one-third less television.

Going hand in hand with falling circulation has been a falling faith in newspapers. A poll by the *Los Angeles Times Mirror* showed reader confidence in newspapers dropping from 51 per cent in 1988 to 24 per cent six years later. In a comment to the *Toronto Star*, Canadian media critic and technological guru Jesse Hirsh said, "The credibility of mainstream media is subverted totally because people now realize they want diversity of thought in order to find out where they stand. The action of an authoritative source like a newspaper telling you the news of the day is gone."

"Competitive pressures become more life-threatening each day," said Nancy Hicks Maynard, the former co-owner and publisher of the *Oakland Tribune* in California, when she was chairwoman of the Freedom Forum Foundation's Media Studies Center in New York. Warning against a bunker mentality, Maynard says, "If journalists insist on doing things as we always have, and if we don't allow new technologies to help us do our jobs better, we'll become irrelevant – lost in cyberspace."

"The big, big change is the Internet," says Dean Singleton, president of MediaNews, a group of 137 American newspapers, including the *Denver Post*. "There is no question the Internet will probably be the biggest change in news dissemination in one hundred years," he says.

One approach being used to meet the impact of the new media is the tailoring of newspaper editions to particular interests. This specialization in news for individual tastes signals the downturn of mass marketing and the beginning of micro marketing. Geographic split runs, where magazines and newspapers drop into a special section articles of interest to a particular area, have been around for years. But now some newspapers are moving towards tailoring papers for, say, those who want business and sports but little else, or those who want entertainment news with only a smidgen of political news. Most publishers talk about keeping a "core" section of news, which would accompany whatever special sections the reader ordered.

"Micro-zoning" for different geographic and demographic markets gives advertisers a more targeted audience and gives readers more of what they've indicated they want. "Micro marketing is an absolute reality, and it's only accelerating as a result of things like the Internet," says American newspaper ad executive Lawrence Sackett. "The ability to pinpoint specific consumers based on demographic lifestyle characteristics . . . flat out works. If we see ourselves as only a mass medium . . . we'll go out of business."

This specialization of subject matter has already happened to magazines, radio, and television, and newspapers are only now catching up. New presses give publishers the technical ability to start and stop printing quickly and even to change plates while the press is running.

The big danger in all this made-to-measure news – a kind of *Daily Me* – is that while it may enrich a person's specific knowledge, it has the potential to fragment society further as it emphasizes individual, not common, interests.

The biggest worry of all for newspaper owners is advertising. It provides about 80 per cent of the income of most newspapers in the States (although in Canada it averages just under that figure), but for some years, this revenue has been under attack from television, and now advertisers are sharply increasing their presence on the Internet. While newspaper profits have soared in the last few years, the long-term trend shows that newspapers' share of total spending on advertising in the United States has been dropping at a rate estimated by the American Press Institute to be 0.05 per cent a year. In Canada, the newspapers' share of total advertising fell from 1990 to 1996 by about the same rate. Both TV, including the new specialty channels, and the Internet are looking hungrily at the newspapers' annual ad revenue in the United States of about $45 billion and the Canadian daily newspaper ad revenue of about $2.3 billion. Thirty years ago, Canadian newspapers had two and a half times the ad revenue of TV, but in the last few years, TV has caught up with newspapers.

Increasingly, advertisers, especially those searching for niche markets, are using direct mail, TV specialty channels, and other vehicles including the Internet to deliver to them a more sharply defined set of potential customers. This, too, is part of mass becoming micro. As well, television has syphoned off a great deal of national advertising from newspapers, making them more reliant on local advertisers.

Today, newspapers face a new adversary in the Internet,

where ad revenue, while still relatively modest in volume, is increasing at a phenomenal rate. In the United States, on-line advertising brought in about $12 million in 1994, $55 million in 1995, $266 million in 1996, and, according to the Internet Advertising Bureau, about $900 million in 1997. Canadian Internet advertising proportionately lags far behind the United States so far, with the estimate for 1997 of just under $10 million. The Internet Advertising Bureau of Canada forecasts nearly $23 million in 1998 and $57 million in 1999. The U.S. figure will leap to $5 billion by 2000, according to Jupiter Communications, a New York research firm. A study by Forrester Research Inc. of Cambridge, Massachusetts, estimates that within three years, newspapers will lose more than 10 per cent of their total ad revenue to on-line media.

Particularly vulnerable are the newspapers' crown jewels, classified ads, a $17-billion-a-year business for American papers and about a $650-million business for Canadian papers. They represent about a third of ad revenue for most daily papers, but within a decade or so, much of that may well have gone to cyberspace.

"Electronic classifieds are a threat," says *Toronto Star* president David Galloway. "We cannot pretend they are not." That's why, he says, newspapers such as the *Star* are moving heavily onto the Web.

The Knight-Ridder newspaper chain CEO Tony Ridder told an Associated Press conference, "The industry's number-one priority has to be to protect the classified franchise in print and extend it on-line." Knight-Ridder spent $27 million in 1997 on its thirty-two Web sites.

Bill Bass, a senior media analyst at Forrester Research, says on-line classifieds cost about a third of newspaper classifieds. He forecasts that large non-newspaper Web entrepreneurs will ultimately capture about 70 per cent of classified-ad revenues from newspapers. Indeed, fear of losing classified ads is one of the strongest forces driving newspapers on-line. The Newspaper Association of America has estimated that if there were a 50 per cent loss of classifieds, the profit margin for the average paper would drop from 14 per cent to 3 per cent, and a 70 per cent loss of classifieds would mean that they'd basically be losing money.

Newspaper automobile ads are also in danger from the Internet. Auto companies now offer Web sites where customers can specify the make, model, and features they want and quickly get price quotes and financing arrangements from dealers. Web-site dealers figure they make more profit and save customers hundreds, if not thousands, of dollars because of the Internet's lower advertising, sales, and commission costs. The Ford Motor Company of Canada Ltd. says a thousand people a day use its Web sites, and General Motors of Canada expects that all of its nine hundred dealers will soon have their own Web sites. Chrysler, the first American automaker to go on-line in 1995, forecasts that 25 per cent of all its car sales will be via the Internet within four years. Microsoft head Bill Gates says 1 per cent of all cars sold in the United States are now sold through the Internet, and he expects that figure to increase dramatically in the near future. The *Washington Post* and *Los Angeles Times* have struck back with a joint effort to advertise both new and used cars on-line.

Books are also becoming big sellers on the Internet. Amazon, the world's largest on-line bookstore, with 2.5 million titles, had sales of $148 million in 1997. In Canada, a Website partnership of Chapters and the *Globe and Mail*, planned to start in late 1998, will offer 2 million titles for sale and will include *Globe and Mail* book reviews and commentaries.

Total Internet book sales in North America have been forecast at $400 million for 1998.

One key attraction for on-line bookstores is that readers can buy a book for up to 40 per cent less than in a store because sales on the Internet are much cheaper to handle.

On-line real-estate ads are also increasingly popular and threatening to newspapers. They offer pictures of homes for sale and offices and apartments for rent, and have much the same interactivity as the car Web sites. To counter media new-comers who are exploiting this market, the *Los Angeles Times Mirror* has made a major investment in "Listing Link," a real-estate Web site that offers more than two hundred thousand listings across the United States. Other papers are following, trying to catch up with new media companies already harvesting the field.

"Failure to protect classified . . . will result in loss of the entire classified business," Conrad Black told a Calgary conference on the future of newspapers in late 1997. "We do not intend to sit like suet puddings and allow this to happen to us." An increasing number of papers, including Black's, now put their classified ads on their own Web sites, some free of charge, some for a small, additional fee. The *Globe and Mail* has developed an interactive job advertising service, based on its highly profitable "Careers" newspaper section and financed by a 3 per cent increase in price. Clients can key in to the on-line ads and ask for more information.

In the United States, the *New York Times*, the *Los Angeles Times*, the *Washington Post*, and about twenty-five other papers have created an on-line site called "CareerPath," which links employers and job seekers. In Canada, Ottawa-based CareerBridge says it is getting 60,000 hits a day on its Web site of job opportunities. The service is free to job-seekers and costs companies $6,000 to $10,000 to put their openings on the site. In the United States, Career Mosaic, a giant non-newspaper employment site, receives 350,000 job queries each day. It's estimated by the Internet Business Network in California that by the end of 1998 there will be 20,000 career sites on the Web with millions of jobs offered or sought.

Some newspapers, including the *Globe and Mail*, also put their personal ads on the Internet. What the American papers, the *Globe and Mail*, the Southam papers, the *Sun* papers, and others are doing is making a pre-emptive strike before Internet newcomers walk away with classified ads and other newspaper advertising. "Staying still is not just staying still," says *Globe and Mail* publisher Roger Parkinson. "It's sinking."

Sensing the newspapers' vulnerability, a lot of the newcomers are moving in not only on classified ads, real-estate, automobile, and entertainment ads, but also moving in editorially on sports scores and theatre, restaurant, stock-market, concert, and TV listings and reviews, and a host of other information. On the Internet, you can find out where to play golf or skate and click to a map showing you how to get there. Companies are moving onto the Web with on-line city guides, hoping to become the principal locale for notification of entertainment and community events. Some provide news on their own and some in alliance with community newspapers or local broadcasters. Bill Gates's Microsoft Network has Web sites for autos, travel, and real estate complete with ads, news stories, and features. Just about every major American city has such Web sites, and Canadian cities are now getting the same kind of service, including a Microsoft site called "Newsview," which offers less text and more visuals than most other news sites. The majority of these services are provided by non-newspaper companies, creeping into what up until now has been largely newspaper territory. CBS has begun trying to capture classified, auto-motive, real-estate, and employment advertising via Web sites at its owned and affiliated stations across the United States. Newspapers, such as the *Toronto Star*, are counteracting these moves by starting their own on-line services that provide infor-mation about what is going on in the city. The *Star* and the *Toronto Sun* have gone even further with their own local twenty-four-hour information TV channel in addition to their Internet sites.

With their advertising revenue under threat, their readers becoming viewers, and even their basic *raison d'être* being hijacked by the electronic media, newspapers face the toughest fight for survival in their history despite current high profits. The reaction of many papers in Canada and the United States has been to put on their war paint, cut news budgets, cut staff, cut the "news hole" (the space devoted to news), and add colour and new layouts. Scared by television, newspapers have killed off the bulk of their afternoon editions, and news stories are getting shorter, simpler, less serious, more entertaining – all toes but no legs.

At the same time, a drive for higher profits has led to a sulky disenchantment in the newsrooms. Journalists have grimly watched the cut-backs, sometimes executed with surprising brutality, as happened at the Saskatoon *StarPhoenix*, the Regina *Leader-Post*, and even the CBC and CTV. Newspapers and news agencies around the world have been reducing staff and cutting research and travel budgets. The Southam chain cut its staff by about one-quarter. United Press International is a shadow of its former self after wholesale dismissals in its domestic service and closing most of its European bureaus. Canadian Press has crept back from near death, but it now offers a thinner version of its previous service. It cut back its original reporting dramatically and focuses on distributing stories provided by its newspaper owners. Its Ottawa bureau has been reduced by about one-half. The CBC news staff reductions have also affected the quality of its functions, for instance, reducing its own coverage of distant events and issues, as have cut-backs at private stations.

There is grouchiness, too, in the newsroom because journalists who have hung on to their jobs have been obliged to take on multi-skilling, doing the jobs of several people. Some TV reporters not only do their usual news stories, they now have to run their own cameras and their own sound, and do their own lighting and technical editing. Today a newspaper editor not only edits copy, but also has to focus on layout, typefaces, headline writing, photos, and graphics. For many newspapers, this multi-skilling not only saves money, but it also reflects their growing preoccupation with the packaging of the news over its content. Significantly less time devoted to substance and more to style cannot result in better journalism.

In talking with reporters and editors in newsrooms in Vancouver, Toronto, New York, and Washington, I have heard the same lament about an inhospitable environment and have seen journalists who were once idealists become sceptical, even downright cynical, illustrating the comment in the 1971 Davey Report that Canadian newsrooms were becoming "boneyards of broken dreams." It's true in the United States, as well. "I can't recall a time when we've had as much discontent in our newsrooms, and that goes from the top editor on down," says John Finneman, senior associate director of the American Press

Institute. Reporters and editors, says Eugene Roberts, former managing editor of the *New York Times* and now a professor of journalism at the University of Maryland, are increasingly "disheartened, disenchanted, and disillusioned." It brings to mind the remark about book writers by Canadian communications philosopher Harold Innis, who said that in years gone by "publishers were said to drink toasts to prosperity out of the skulls of authors."

Editor and Publisher says that today most journalists feel a lack of editorial leadership and plan to be out of the business in five or ten years. By then, the magazine says, they believe newspapers will have a less important role to play in society than they do today. But in fact, the flood of information on the Internet has made the role of the journalist more important than ever before in sorting out what is valid and what is not. Whatever its cause, despondency in the newsroom is perhaps the biggest danger of all for newspapers, because the newsroom is the heart and soul of the organization. If newspaper companies are to survive and thrive in whatever form, the thrust will have to come from vibrant, creative, thoughtful professionals in the newsrooms. Without the commitment of journalists, the new media predators will have newspaper barons such as Conrad Black, Ken Thomson, Rupert Murdoch, and Katharine Graham for breakfast.

"In the end," says Eugene Roberts, "you have to have a news hole, you have to have a travel budget, you have to make some kind of financial commitment to underpin the skills of these journalists. And that's what's beginning to slide – plummet in some cases – in newspaper after newspaper."

But many publishers eyeing the immediate bottom line are critical of journalists for putting their standards of editorial credibility and integrity ahead of economic realities. Journalists, they say, must become customer-focused marketers. In an effort to increase advertising revenue, the Thomson papers in the United States and Canada are placing ads on the front page, something that has generally been considered taboo for generations. "We're not sacrificing our journalistic virginity just because we're putting advertising on the front page," says Stuart Garner, head of the Thomson papers. In a speech to the International Newspaper Marketing Association in 1997, Garner said, "It makes me angry to see complacency in lots of newspaper departments, particularly among editors and journalists sitting in ivory towers believing they're on God's work and above all this marketing stuff. God's work it may be, but God didn't give them the right to bore the pants off readers."

Conrad Black, the world's third-largest newspaper publisher, agrees. "My experience with journalists authorizes me to record that a very large number of them are ignorant, lazy, opinionated, intellectually dishonest, and inadequately supervised," he once said. There is, he says, "too much sanctimonious talk about the sacred trust of the journalist." Black also worries about "the insane segregation of commercial and editorial management," as does Phoenix, Arizona, newspaper publisher John Oppendahl. "Editors increasingly are going to have to turn into marketers," Oppendahl says. "They may not want to admit it, but they're going to have to."

This approach has been adopted by the *Los Angeles Times*, which has done more than any other major North American daily paper to marry its editorial and business sides. Its objective is to increase circulation and advertising, but journalists fear that the editorial side will increasingly be working in close proximity to people preoccupied by ad revenues, not editorial quality and independence. Already *L.A. Times* editors have been asked to do stories favourable to advertisers. It's a long way from the days when Henry Luce protected the editorial independence of *Time* magazine by keeping news and advertising apart in a "church and state" division of departments.

Another factor affecting the nature of news is the advent of focus-group journalism, which gives the customers what they say they want, not necessarily what they need to know as citizens. It has led to more "visual" print journalists: designers, illustrators, artists, photographers, editors, and reporters all attuned to what catches the eye more than what feeds the mind.

But there are dissenters. "When you design papers for people who don't read, you alienate those who do and you don't attract those who don't," says Tom Rosenstiel, director of the Project for Excellence in Journalism, an American media-research organization.

You can see that happening in many newspapers today as they look for ways to retain their increasingly distracted readers by restyling their pages with more photographs, more colour, more white space, larger, brighter type, snazzier headlines, more graphics seeking to encapsulate complicated stories, and writing that lands a punch in every paragraph. Much of this can be valuable, especially when it is used to enhance quality journalism. The "good grey lady" of journalism, the *New York Times*, has been dressed up in colour and new lifestyle sections to make the paper more touchy-feely and less fuddy-duddy. The *Globe and Mail* is making the same kinds of changes, largely out of fear of competition from Conrad Black's new national paper. A Canadian, Lucie Lacava of Montreal, is a world-class newspaper redesigner who has created new looks for many Canadian papers, such as the *Ottawa Citizen* and the Montreal *Gazette*. Lacava's aim is not so much to entice those who don't read newspapers, but to make it easier, less cluttered for those who do.

Redesigning the layout just to look different, however, is something else, as is the marketing-induced trend to publish "soft" features, contests, how-to articles, shorter and fewer stories on political, social, and economic issues and on controversial events in general. What's trendy today is happy news, personality news, crime news, and sensationalism. The objective is to please as many readers and to offend as few as possible. But any effort that cheapens the news for the sake of using new gadgets and techniques is doomed to failure in the long run.

As history bears out, junkyard journalism has always been with us. Never, however, has it been so widespread and popular, nor so infectious for mainstream media, as it is today. The British tabloids, such as *News of the World*, the *Star*, or the *Sun*, long ago proved that sex and scandal were an exciting and profitable combination, and their style has been borrowed and enriched by the tabloids flooding North American supermarket racks.

Offering a mix of Hollywood gossip, quack cancer cures, sordid crime, innumerable sightings of monsters, aliens, and Elvis, the supermarket tabloids, led by the *National Enquirer*, have been regarded in recent years as almost respectable. Editors at major newspapers and TV networks, who previously scorned the tabloids' Peeping Tom journalism, now carefully read them for potential news items. "The tide is running in the direction of lowest common denominator journalism, and that is very sad," says Marvin Kalb, director of Harvard University's Center on the Press, Politics and Public Policy.

What worries many serious journalists is not so much the excesses of the supermarket tabloids, but rather the growing influence they have on the mainstream media. The "tabs" are not yet setting the news agenda, but they are distorting it. Mainstream editors now worry that if they don't carry a revealing if factually questionable story, their competitors will. Many a front-page article now originates with the tabloids. Even the venerable *New York Times* has been, at times, seduced by sensationalism, quoting the *National Enquirer* as a news source in reports on the O. J. Simpson case. The *Enquirer*, according to the *Times's* Los Angeles bureau chief David Margolick, "probably shaped public perception of the [Simpson] case more than any other publication."

At the height of its coverage of this story, the *National Enquirer* saw its weekly circulation increase by five hundred thousand copies. Its editor, Steve Coz, has boasted that mainstream news publications are now following his paper's style, especially in their coverage of celebrities. "That's the *Enquirer's* influence, whether you like it or don't like it," he says. Coz, a Harvard graduate, was named by *Time* magazine as one of the most influential people of 1997.

California Governor Pete Wilson was so alarmed about jurors and witnesses selling exclusive information to the *National Enquirer* and similar "tabs" that, during the O. J. Simpson case, he signed three new laws providing penalties for doing so. The "tabs" pay heavily for juicy news tidbits, although Coz says he paid "under $100,000" for the first paparazzi photographs of Madonna's baby. He did pay $100,000, though, for Nicole Simpson's diaries. Her maid was paid $18,000 for her memories of the tumultuous Simpson marriage. The TV show *A Current Affair* paid $162,500 for videos and photos of the Simpson wedding. The tabloid the *Globe* offered $500,000 for evidence leading to a conviction in the murder of six-year-old JonBenet Ramsey in Colorado. The *National Enquirer* offered the girl's family $1 million if they would take a lie detector test. In another case, the *Enquirer* offered a $100,000 reward for leads to the killer of comedian Bill Cosby's son. Big money has been paid in Britain, too, for sensational stories. The *News of the World* paid around £44,000 for the diaries and confessions of society playgirl Christine Keeler in the 1960s. Owner Rupert Murdoch dismissed criticism of this payout, saying, "People can sneer as much as they like, but I'll take the 150,000 extra copies we're going to sell."

The American tabloids provided the editorial lead on other stories later picked up by mainstream media – the William Kennedy Smith rape charges; the political scandal of Clinton White House aide Dick Morris; the news that Lorena Bobbitt had chopped off her husband's penis; the accusations of sexual misconduct against President Clinton and Michael Jackson. The mainstream media also ran the story of sports hero and broadcaster Frank Gifford frolicking in a hotel bedroom with a woman whom the *Globe* tabloid had paid $75,000 for a story on her fling with Gifford. Shortly before the deaths of Princess Diana and "Dodi" al-Fayed, the tabloids were offering huge amounts of money for intimate photos of the couple. The *Globe* paid $210,000 for shots of them in their bathing suits. After the fatal car crash in Paris, photos of the death scene reportedly were being offered for $1 million. Germany's *Bild Zeitung* paid "a lot," its editor said, for pictures it published of two crumpled bodies in the wreckage of the car.

A public outcry against the intrusive coverage of Princess Diana, and professional embarrassment, led the British tabloids to agree on a code of ethics to protect people's privacy. The very day that code was announced, however, the "tabs" emblazoned their front pages with stories of a supposed last interview with Diana that had been carried by *Paris Match*. "Our Love by Diana and Dodi," screamed the *Mirror*, which also featured intimate, long-lens photos of Diana and "Dodi," the very type of picture the new ethical code was supposed to bar. "My Dream of Happiness. Diana's Amazing Last Interview Revealed Her Love For Dodi," read the *Sun*'s headline. Even such august London papers as the *Daily Telegraph* and the *Times* front-paged the "interview" although they questioned its legitimacy, noting that the *Paris Match* article carried no byline.

There are many other instances of the tabloid infection of the mainstream media. Newspapers in Europe and North America ran lurid headlines over their stories on the romantic escapades and sexy phone calls of Prince Charles and Camilla Parker-Bowles. They published photos of a topless Duchess of York having her toes sucked by an admirer, as well as stories on Eddie Murphy's dalliance with a transvestite prostitute. Even the BBC pulled correspondents out of assignments in the Middle East to cover the sensational divorce case in South Africa of Diana's brother, Earl Spencer.

The mainstream media's focus on the sex lives of American politicians accelerated about a decade ago when news stories forced Senator Gary Hart out of the Democratic presidential nomination race in 1988 after the *National Enquirer* published photos of Hart snuggling up with Donna Rice aboard a yacht appropriately named *Monkey Business*. Nothing, however, could match the media firestorm in the initial coverage of the alleged affair between President Clinton and a White House intern.

"The basic interests of the human race are not in music, politics, and philosophy, but in things like food and football, money and sex and crime – especially crime," says Larry Lamb, the editorial director of the *Sun* and the *News of the World* in Britain. Educating the public is the last thing tabloid editors want to do.

Tom Rosenstiel, who prior to heading an organization that researches journalism was a long-time Washington correspondent for *Newsweek*, says he was told by a senior colleague at the magazine, "We once used to edit this magazine by reading the *New York Times* Thursday morning. Today, we edit the magazine by reading the front page of the [tabloid] *New York Post* Thursday morning and the fax edition of the supermarket *Star*."

"In search of audience," Rosenstiel says, "we routinely print unsubstantiated rumour on the justification that it's already out there. We lack the courage of our former convictions of what is news. We fear if we live up to our standards, we'll be perceived as élitist or irrelevant."

A growing number of newspapers are beginning to live up to British writer Claud Cockburn's comment that "the journalist is partly in the entertainment business and partly in the advertising business." Or, as writer and editor H. L. Mencken once said, "A newspaper is a device for making the ignorant more ignorant and the crazy, crazier."

Canadians buy the supermarket "tabs" as enthusiastically as Americans, each week purchasing more than 200,000 *National Enquirers* and about 100,000 copies of the *Globe*. We have had only moderate success, however, with our own versions, publications such as *Hush* and *Flash*, although in Quebec the "tabs" are very popular. The gossip weekly *Frank*, while not as bizarre as the American tabloids, is crueller and is read assiduously by journalists and politicians looking for gossip, but hoping not to find their own names in it. In the first two decades of the twentieth century, the Calgary *Eye Opener* under the direction of its exuberant editor, Bob Edwards, successfully specialized in political satire and gossip.

The most successful Canadian examples of tabloid journalism are the *Sun* newspapers, particularly the *Toronto Sun*, with its screeching front-page headlines: "Insane Strangler a Time Bomb in Toronto"; "Why Should This Junkie Cop-Killer Go Free?" It publishes sexually tantalizing pictures of Sunshine Girls and Boys, gossip, features such as "Fun," "Money," "Showbiz," "Lifestyle," "Travel," sharply opinionated columnists, abbreviated news stories, and a sense of streetwise, blue-collar involvement. It certainly has worked for the *Sun*. "The Little Paper That Grew" is one of the marketing marvels of North American journalism.

USA Today, which began in the early 1980s, today is the leading national American daily paper, with a circulation of about 2 million. It epitomizes the new, consumer-friendly style that seems to shout out "Have A Nice Day!" It was designed to attract the TV generation, with short articles and big, colourful graphics. It has had a greater impact on newspaper style than anything else in this century in North America. The *Globe and Mail* has recently borrowed its approach to some degree because, says Stuart Garner of the Thomson papers, the *Globe* lacked "*élan*." Even Conrad Black has borrowed a few ideas from *USA Today*, although he proclaimed that his new paper would be "much more high quality" than *USA Today*, which he describes as "middle market."

Another paper that presents the news as fun is the *Mercury News* in San Jose, California, which devotes a weekly section to success stories written by readers. It also taps into readers' emotions with regular features such as "How I Met My True Love" and "The Seven-Second Philosopher." The *Pittsburgh Post-Gazette* has been experimenting with a Sunday front page that has no news on it at all, just highlights of features inside. Even the *Toronto Star* now describes itself as "the friendlier, reader-relevant giant." If these are trends, as they seem to be, then it's further evidence that the role of journalist as teacher is clearly giving way to journalist as entertainer.

The tarting up of a newspaper's look and content threatens to overshadow its fundamental educational role. Decades ago, reflecting on the ever-present conflict between making a profit and delivering the news, Eugene Meyer, the owner of the *Washington Post*, said, "To survive, a newspaper must be a commercial success. At the same time, a newspaper has a relation to the public interest which is different from other commercial enterprises. . . . The citizens of a free country have to depend on a free press for the information necessary to the intelligent discharge of their duties of citizenship."

These days, however, in an increasing number of cases, the marketing tail is starting to wag the editorial dog. But if newspapers, in their struggle to survive in an Internet world, become largely merchants of diverting entertainment, they will always come out second best to the real entertainers on television: the talk-show hosts and the infotainment personalities, as well as the comedians, singers, and actors.

It's one thing to dress up the news pages to make the important stories more interesting and relevant, but it's another to make papers more entertaining, more exciting, more colourful, more sensational, purely as a marketing device to meet advertisers' desires, focus-group reactions, and competition from the new electronic media.

A lot of newspapers have not survived the changing marketplace. More than 150 daily papers in the United States have died in the last twenty-five years – about seventy since 1991 – and in Canada the number of daily newspapers has fallen from 120 in 1980 to 105 by 1998. This makes Conrad Black's launch of a new national daily an impressive, daredevil act.

Fear of the new media and a lessening interest in owning papers in the second and third generation has encouraged family-owned papers to sell out to chains and groups, such as Conrad Black's or, in the United States, MediaNews and Knight-Ridder. Independent and family papers may soon be a thing of the past. Even greater concentration of ownership in the United States will happen if the chains are successful in getting rid of government rules limiting cross-ownership of papers and broadcasting operations. "When that happens, consolidation will be tremendous," says Dean Singleton. He thinks it's possible that in a decade, almost all of the fifteen hundred papers in the United States will be run by ten corporations. The process of consolidation puts the control of newspapers into the hands of fewer and fewer people. In Canada, this concentration of ownership has already happened, with Conrad Black controlling so many Canadian daily papers. The fear of such concentration of ownership is that Black, with his enormous power, could dominate any public debate, squeezing out opinions contrary to his ideological bent. While he may have that potential and while his editorials do reflect his conservative politics, nevertheless for the most part the news in his papers has been largely free from bias.

If a jazzier appearance is no solution to the challenges confronting daily papers, and if the daily news is more quickly and readily available on radio, TV, and the Internet, what's the newspaper to do? Basically, newspaper survival will involve three things: playing to strength; reinventing the newspaper; and going electronic.

Playing to strength means doing what they can do better than anyone else: gathering, editing, orchestrating the news, separating what's important from what's not, what's true from what's not. It means recapturing the role of journalist as a brand-name navigator and teacher and shedding the gaudy clothes of the entertainer. "We must explain not only why, but what does it mean and what is coming next," says *Financial Times* chairman David Bell, who adds, "Editors are a vital function of democracy." Now that the news of what's happening is already known to most people by the time they get to their paper, newspapers need to be more reflective than immediate, less *news*papers and more background and commentary papers, in a way, moving into the role previously occupied by newsmagazines.

"In the future, it's not news you'll be looking for, it's context. And that's what brand-name publishers will provide – content and context," says Lib Gibson of the Globe and Mail Information Services, whose motto is "Where information becomes intelligence."

A few editors have taken this route, spurning the bells, whistles, and froth and going up market with more analytical, background, explanatory stories. The *Ottawa Citizen* has taken that approach in a much publicized reworking of the paper, and it has paid off at least modestly. Early figures show about a 2 per cent circulation increase for 1997 over the previous year. Others that have taken the quality route include the *Globe and Mail* in Toronto, the *New York Times*, and in London, the *Independent*, the *Times*, and the *Daily Telegraph*. Conrad Black says traditional values are critical to success. "A well-edited newspaper with an intelligent selection of news, features, sports, business, and comment becomes more important than ever, as the media consumer contemplates the alternatives of swimming upstream against a cascading torrent of undifferentiated transmissions."

"Our future," says Tom Rosenstiel, "lies . . . in traditional standards of news and . . . the purpose of the craft. . . . That sense of purpose and potential and virtue that attracted some of the best of the last two generations into journalism is disappearing and a sense of crisis has replaced it. . . . The question is not simply, Will newspapers survive? It's also, Should they?"

"We must differentiate ourselves . . . from TV, and that means more and better explanation journalism, more context, more meaning, more meat," Sandra Mims Rowe, president of the American Society of Newspaper Editors, said at a seminar in Washington, D.C., on the future of newspapers. Eugene Roberts, former managing editor of the *New York Times*, heartily endorses that approach, saying, "A good newspaper will lead, not ingratiate; challenge, not pacify; educate not edify; explain, not avoid."

Reinvention involves a sharp division between local and national papers. Local papers need to focus primarily on local news almost to the exclusion of national and international news, which is readily available elsewhere. Reinvention also means national papers need to concentrate on national and world issues, providing insight, context, and background designed to make complex stories relevant and understandable. Reinvention means concentrating, perhaps in time exclusively, on the Saturday and Sunday editions. On weekends, readers have the time and inclination to browse and think, and so weekend editions can provide a "resting place" for words, as McLuhan program head Derrick de Kerckhove has said. The Canadian Newspaper Association says the average Canadian newspaper reader today spends about forty-five minutes a day with the papers on weekdays, but an hour and a half on weekends. Indeed, two new Sunday papers began in 1998 in Halifax and London, Ontario, seeking to exploit this inclination. Within a generation, most Monday-to-Friday papers could go totally on the Internet through the week and on paper on the weekend.

Going electronic is an increasingly necessary and viable option for newspapers. The number of Canadians with access to the Internet doubled between 1996 and 1997, and by the end of 1998 about 20 per cent of Canadian homes will be on-line and nearly 50 per cent shortly after 2000. In 1997, 36 per cent of Canadian homes had computers, 4.1 million of them, and the numbers rise every year.

The technological revolution is illustrated by the growing traffic on the Internet. It is doubling every hundred days according to the U.S. Commerce Department. In the face of the new and aggressive electronic competitors, newspapers must change or die. "When competitors move in on us, we should not cut quality . . . in a foolhardy effort to keep up short-term profit margins," says Eugene Patterson, Pulitzer Prize-winner and recent editor and president of Florida's *St. Petersburg Times*. "When the 'beasties' first say, 'Boo!' we shouldn't wail, quit, and run. We should adapt, act, and dominate."

The Internet is a terrifying threat to the future of newspapers. At the same time, it's a golden opportunity for those willing to change. "Newspapers will benefit from being bedfellows with the Internet," says *Toronto Star* president David Galloway. For news to "adapt, act, and dominate" will mean taking advantage of the Internet's immediacy and its ability to combine picture, sound, and text with a large element of interactivity. It's the "mediamorphosis" that futurist Roger Fidler has talked about.

Essentially it means that thriving newspapers will become multiproduct information companies, gathering, organizing, and putting in context the news of the day and distributing it via a number of "pipelines." This is not going to happen tomorrow, but we're on the way. "We will dominate the Internet big-time," boasts William Singleton, head of MediaNews Group. "The information revolution belongs to us."

The news companies that succeed will become "information centres," providing news primarily via the Internet, but on paper on weekends, in specialized newsletters to targeted groups, by operating weekly community and suburban papers, and through other custom services on the Internet, such as interactive entertainment and classified ads, job, real-estate, car, mutual-fund, and stock-market listings, and a whole range of tailored services.

"We will provide our content however our customers want it, on newsprint, on screens, on fax machines, or towed around in large letters behind blimps overhead," says Conrad Black, noting that his newspapers have more than seventy Web sites around the world with millions of so-called hits a day. "If . . . the content is good, the means of delivery is secondary," he says.

But the cyberworld holds perils for journalism, API president William Winter says. "There has been an increasingly anxious debate about . . . what role . . . will traditional newsroom values such as accuracy, thoroughness, and impartiality play in online versions of today's print newspapers. Can those values survive, or will they perish, as has so much else of substance in an age in which surface flash seems so often to be favoured over real depth?"

Right now, the Internet is awash with amateurs, charlatans, political "spinners," conspiracy addicts, and questionable "experts" all offering "news" through chat groups and individual Web sites, making the Internet a hotbed of rumour, speculation, and conspiracy theories. In 1996, the *American Journalism Review* reported on how an on-line newspaper, the *American Reporter*, carried a story of a possible Chinese nuclear attack on the United States, alarming millions who saw it. After the crash of TWA Flight 800 off Long Island in 1996, conspiracy theorists were almost instantly on the Internet with reports that the plane had been shot down by terrorists or by the U.S. military. Web conspiracy theorists variously claim that Princess Diana was murdered by the CIA, by the British Secret Service on orders from the Queen, by the Rockefellers, or by the Rothschilds.

Typical of far-out journalism on the Web has been the work of a wanna-be Walter Winchell by the name of Matt Drudge. He's a thirty-two-year-old cyber-muckraker in Hollywood, who posts on the Internet the *Drudge Report*, a daily digest of media gossip liberally laced with his own comments and allegations about spousal abuse, alcoholism, sexual harassment, criminal activities, and even murder by public figures. (In Ottawa, there is the *Bourque NewsWatch*, a more informative and less flamboyant Web site, offering inside political reports.) Drudge is not hampered by concepts such as journalistic integrity, fairness, or balance. Caught in one error, he tried to cover himself by saying, "At worst, it was an accurate report of an inaccurate rumour." The numbers of visitors to his Web site zoomed when he was among the first to carry the sexual allegations about President Clinton and a White House intern. Like his idol Winchell, Drudge's journalistic philosophy is, as he told the NBC's *Today* show, "I go where the stink is." Attracted by such journalistic values, the Rupert Murdoch Fox News channel hired him to host a weekend news program.

Not to be outdone, radio's lewdest, crudest voice, Howard Stern, has gone into television with a syndicated show to be aired by CBS-owned stations and others. Announcing his new TV infotainment show, Stern said, "Television has changed. Standards have gone down to an all-time low, and I'm here to represent it."

With brand-name quality, newspapers on the Internet can chase away much of this hyperventilated so-called news. Most people have neither the skill nor the time to evaluate the endless amount of news on the Web and need navigators they can trust to take them through the day's events. Some Internet purists argue that this would remove much of the increased democracy that the Internet provides, putting citizens back into the hands of agenda-setting editors with their values and judgements. Nonsense! What it would do is limit journalistic anarchy and irresponsibly speculative news and increase reliability, stability, and integrity. Individual news Web sites and chat groups would still exist, but you would have the opportunity to get the news from dependable sources.

Many publishers have been hesitant to jump onto the Internet. Some echo the attitude of Emperor Franz Joseph, who said back in the late 1800s about the new technology of flush toilets, "It begins with water closets and ends with revolution."

Even as far-sighted a publisher as Conrad Black sees a continuing role for ink and paper newspapers. "I may be a nostalgic sentimentalist," he has said, "but I have a feeling that some people will continue to want to be able to tuck a newspaper under their arms to read on the subway, or wherever, for a long time." Probably they will, in decreasing numbers, but likely not much beyond the next twenty years.

New York Times chairman emeritus Arthur Ochs Sulzberger, Jr., whose paper is highly active on the Internet, notes how much cheaper it would be to have the *Times* totally on the Internet instead of on paper. "The Internet, in my judgement, while it's going to be some years before it's a huge success, offers us a way of distributing our information at tremendously low costs. No more worrying about pricing on paper. No more worrying about trucking costs. No more worrying about printing and distribution. When that happens – and it's conceivable that it will happen ten, twenty years from now – then we're really only building our business on the back of our journalism."

The prospect of cost-savings on top of the competitive reality that if publishers don't go on-line with electronic news, somebody else will, has spurred newspapers into action. There were 4 U.S. newspapers on-line in 1985, 7 in 1991, 100 in 1994, 2,000 in 1996, and more than 3,000 by 1997. Today it's estimated there are more than 8,000 Web news sites in North America, including papers, TV stations, magazines, city guides, and other on-line media services. Most of Canada's daily newspapers have Web sites; the *Globe and Mail*, the *Toronto Star*, Southam's, and the *Sun* papers all being especially active. In the United States, the *Wall Street Journal*, Reuters, and Associated Press are major Internet news providers, as are hundreds of local newspapers. The Newspaper Association of America says that in 1997 one-third of newspapers responding to its enquiries reported that they're beginning to make money on the Net.

Internet news groups such as CNN Interactive, MSNBC Online, and ABCNEWS.com are TV-owned news services that have the advantage of video resources and know-how, which will be invaluable with the convergence of the Web and TV. PointCast, with more than 1.1 million active users in the United States and 75,000 in Canada, is another news giant on the Web, providing news and a wide range of entertainment, business, and sports reports as well as stock-market information. Canoe, Canadian Online Explorer, operated by Sun Media, has more than doubled its business every year. It had more than 1 million page hits when it posted the news of the death of Princess Diana and registers about 30 million page views each month. Canoe also has joined forces with MediaLinX Interactive to establish NetForce, Canada's largest full-service Internet advertising company, working with ad agencies and advertisers.

The Southam papers launched a Web site in the spring of 1998 that claimed to have the most powerful search capacity of any Canadian on-line site. It provides news, weather forecasts, various business services, travel information, and reservation services, TV listings, lottery results, chat groups, and plans to have career and classified advertising and an interactive shopping mall.

Some of these on-line services, such as that of the *Wall Street Journal*, which has more than one hundred thousand users, charge a subscription fee, and some, such as PointCast, are supported solely by advertising.

The *Globe and Mail* made its first move to the electronic age in the 1970s when it transformed itself into a national daily by the use of satellites that allowed the newspaper same-day delivery across Canada. It was also one of the first newspapers in Canada to go on-line (the first was the Halifax *Daily News*, in 1994). The *Globe* has a large number of electronic tentacles, including an on-line discussion group and an Internet alliance with the business service, Dow Jones. It is also a partner of PointCast, adding its own material to the Canadian service. As well, it is developing a number of specialty sites, such as one for investors that provides only stories about mutual funds.

The Canadian Press, the *Toronto Star,* the *Toronto Sun,* the *Financial Post,* the *Edmonton Journal,* the *Vancouver Sun,* the *Halifax Chronicle-Herald,* and most other Canadian papers as well as the CBC, CTV, and other broadcasters put some or all of their editorial product on-line. CBC AM and FM radio networks have been simulcasting their programming on the Internet since 1996, as have many other stations. CBC Radio can now be heard anywhere in the world via its Web site.

So far, the editorial staffs for Web sites are relatively small at Canadian papers and, with a few exceptions, at most U.S. paper sites, too. As the Internet expands, however, Web staffs will have to grow substantially. The largest Internet news staff is employed by CNN, which has about 170 people devoted to its Web site.

One of the criticisms of the Internet newspaper services has been that most of them are simply regurgitating what's in their paper editions, providing "shovelware" instead of reshaping and enriching material to exploit the capabilities of the Internet. Until recently, there has been a disinclination among most newspapers to, in effect, scoop themselves by letting their electronic service have exclusive stories before the paper itself is on the street. That attitude was supported by the fact that on-line readership is still tiny compared to newspaper readership. It is reminiscent of arguments at CBC-TV about letting Newsworld carry major stories that *The National* had developed exclusively before *The National* was on the air. Many newspapers were reluctant even to update their stories on the Internet for fear it would tip off the opposition as to what new information the papers have.

Jealously guarding scoops may make some sense for

individual programs or newspapers, but it is counter-productive in the new environment. The reality is that news organizations must readjust their thinking to take advantage of the Internet's immediacy as well as its limitless space, which enables news organizations to append to the stories supporting material that likely is not included in the paper editions and newscasts.

A growing number of news organizations (more than a third of American papers) have already accepted that they can no longer hold the news back until publication or airtime. They are becoming news agencies where every second counts. When results of the 1997 Olympic Games in Japan came in, numerous U.S. papers immediately put them on their Web sites, sometimes eight to ten hours ahead of the newspapers hitting the street. And when news was breaking in the winter of 1998 on the sexual allegations about Clinton, the *New York Times*, the *Washington Post*, and the *Los Angeles Times* were constantly updating their Web editions instead of holding back the news for the next day's paper. Similarly, *Newsweek* ran detailed reports on its Web site days before its next issue. The *Dallas Morning News* has found that putting its news on-line hours before the paper hits the street has paid off with larger circulation and increased interest from national advertisers. The higher profile resulting from its constantly updated on-line news presence has made the paper a national player in journalism. Clearly, journalistic integrity demands that news organizations provide the news as soon as they get it, which means it will be posted on the Internet first. So far, most Canadian papers have been hesitant to do this.

Whether they use their Web sites for "shovelware" or for more creative approaches, the newspaper sites are basically on-ramps to the Internet superhighway. In the twenty-first century, without a Web presence, newspapers will be dead ducks, going, in less than one hundred years, from monopoly to primary to secondary to, at best, niche status. Their future depends on moving largely from ink to electrons.

Peering ahead, Microsoft's Bill Gates envisions news kiosks on street corners where you browse the Internet and download the newspapers and magazines you want into your own portable electronic device. He foresees these electronic newsstands being a reality by about 2010. Roger Fidler's concept, which seemed revolutionary when he developed it in 1981, is a flat panel computer, like a small laptop computer, which could be carried in a briefcase and provides specialized access to any Web news service you want. Walt Disney Co. developed its flat panel version for downloading publications in 1996, but any commercial use is at least five or ten years away. In Europe, a version of this, called Newspad, has been developed for downloading the news.

Traditionalists who prefer a news*paper* for its comforting ability to be read anywhere – in front of a roaring fireplace, on a subway, or in a hammock – would find much the same quality in the electronic newspaper except for the rustle of turning pages. With its infinite news hole, the Internet can provide far more details on more news stories than even the most exhaustive newspaper can offer.

Before newspapers can regain their journalistic preeminence, however, the pressures to go down market must be first surmounted. My own sense is that things are going to get worse before they get better. It will be some years before it's generally accepted that junkyard journalism is not going to revive bottom lines for publishers nor, to say the least, their reputations. To survive, let alone thrive, publishers have to focus on quality journalism and imaginatively embrace the new electronic world, becoming an information company, not just a newspaper. If they don't, they'll go the way of the buggy-whip business.

7

"This Peep Show!"

"**W**hy do we need this . . . this peep show!" Winston Churchill snorted in the early postwar days of television.

Churchill's disdain was echoed by the founder of the CBC News Service, Dan McArthur, who thought that television was not to be trusted with so important a matter as the news because TV was too frivolous and phony. That was also the belief of the BBC's director general, Sir William Haley, who felt TV was a totally unacceptable medium for news or political discussion.

Most newspaper publishers were of the opinion that the "boob tube" was purely entertainment for "couch potatoes"; it offered no competition for news, and hence was no threat. One man who differed, however, was Edward R. Murrow, soon to be a giant of broadcast journalism, who first watched TV in Britain when the BBC showed the coronation of King George VI in 1937. The BBC had begun TV broadcasting six months earlier, and this was the first major news event ever carried by television. Watching the ceremony with him in the living room of his London home was another future broadcast news star, Eric Severeid. "That's television," Murrow said to a wide-eyed Severeid. "That's the future, my friend." Half a dozen years later, *Maclean's* was equally enthusiastic, talking of TV as "a front row seat in our home" for what was happening in the world.

Ed Murrow and *Maclean's* were right. With eyes around the world staring at 1.2 billion TV sets, there is no doubt of television's reach. "Never in the history of humankind has there been a medium with the impact of television," says Walter Cronkite.

In 1971, a Canadian Radio-Television and Telecommunications Commission (CRTC) survey showed that 90 per cent of Canadians thought that the TV networks were honest in their presentation of the news. Supporting evidence came from the Kent Royal Commission in the early 1980s, which found that most Canadians believed TV provided news that was the most influential, the most fair, the most believable, and the most essential. If ever a medium had power, TV had it.

Television has made it clear that pictures have more impact on people's judgements than written words. That may or may not be a good thing, depending on the quality of the pictures versus the quality of the written words. There is no doubt, however, that television has the biggest platform. Equally, there should be no doubt that the bigger the platform, the bigger is the responsibility.

As Ed Murrow said in the early years of television, "This instrument can teach, it can illuminate, it can even inspire, but only if human beings are willing to use it to those ends. Otherwise, it is only wires and lights in a box."

In Canada in 1931, when TV was still in the laboratory, its future was glimpsed by editor and commentator William A. Deacon, who told a CBC Radio audience that television "can but hasten the end of the radio as a source of entertainment and of the newspaper as a purveyor of news." Television certainly did end radio's role in broadcasting dramas, variety shows, and most other entertainment, and while it has not ended news-papers, it has overtaken them as the principal source of news for most people.

The slam-bang, nanosecond style of most TV news these days, however, suggests that television is largely failing in its responsibility to citizens to report the news comprehensively. There are exceptions, of course, often at the CBC and the BBC and occasionally at CTV and the American networks, but just as newspapers have gone down market in a desperate attempt to meet competition, so, too, has television. On television, the news business is becoming show business, even more than it has in newspapers. In doing so, TV is returning to its earliest days in the late 1930s when BBC TV featured monkeys, models, sword swallowers, and cooks, as well as singers and actors, but seldom showed any substantial news.

BBC TV formally began in 1936, although there were only four hundred sets in Britain, all in the London area. By 1938, BBC TV was occasionally doing some serious journalism and in that year showed images of Prime Minister Neville Chamberlain returning from Munich and waving a piece of paper signed by Adolf Hitler, which, Chamberlain said, promised "peace in our time." The promise didn't last long, and when Nazi bombs fell on Warsaw on September 1, 1939, the BBC television service was shut down for the duration of the war, stopping in the middle of a Mickey Mouse cartoon. The last words spoken on British TV until mid-1946 were those of Mickey imitating Greta Garbo and saying as the screen went to black, "Ah tink ah go home." When TV resumed after the war,

Mickey Mouse as Garbo was the first show aired. News, however, remained a stepchild at BBC TV. Until 1948, it was read by an anonymous announcer sitting in front of a clock.

In the United States, TV was first seen by large numbers of people in New York when President Franklin Delano Roosevelt opened the New York World's Fair before the cameras in 1939. But through the war years, news was barely an afterthought for American television. In the immediate postwar years, too, the focus was on song, dance, and comedy, highlighted by "Mr. Television," comedian Milton Berle. (Appropriately, for all its magic tricks and mesmerizing performances, the word television was translated into the Algonquin language as "conjuring tent.") The first TV "stars" to anchor the news in the United States, Britain, and Canada were announcers who had no background in journalism. Illustrating the more frivolous attitude taken to TV news at the time was NBC News anchor John Cameron Swayze, who typically introduced international reports with the comment "Now let's go hop-scotching the world for headlines."

News on radio was greeted with derision when it first began in Canada on a national public network in the early 1930s. Broadcast executives reasoned that while radio news might be useful for those living on farms who got their newspapers several days late, it would be of little value for city and town dwellers. The same attitude greeted television when it arrived in Canada two decades later. A few, however, took TV journalism more seriously. In early 1952, when he was training the first CBC-TV producers, Gilbert Seldes, the noted author and a former CBS TV producer, told his young, creative trainees, "We have to wonder what television will do to our intelligence.

It may stimulate us to thought, but it may also put our minds to sleep."

Conventional wisdom at the time was that the "boob tube" would more likely put people to sleep by inducing "passivity of mind" and "spectatoritis," or turn them into "televidiots." *Globe and Mail* associate editor Hamish McGeachy warned that TV would destroy conversation and make thinking obsolete. To suggest at the time of TV's arrival that TV news would come to dominate the dissemination of news was dismissed with the ridiculing comment that TV offered "today's news with yesterday's pictures." Indeed, when CBC was first considering a TV newscast, it was seriously proposed that the 11 P.M. TV newscast should simply show an announcer reading the 10 P.M. radio newscast.

In what he said to his trainees, Gilbert Seldes pinpointed the dilemma facing television news producers: whether to educate or entertain. Determined efforts have been made by broadcast journalists from Edward R. Murrow to Walter Cronkite to Peter Jennings in the United States and from Norman DePoe to Barbara Frum to Peter Mansbridge in Canada to present TV journalism as lively education. Backed by like-minded producers, they demonstrated how thoughtful TV could, indeed, surpass newspapers in impact and power.

Canadian TV led the way in North America in trying to popularize serious journalism with the breakthrough program *This Hour Has Seven Days* in the mid-1960s. Producers Douglas Leiterman and Patrick Watson wanted a public-affairs program that was, as they said, "entertaining and exciting," as well as informative. What they sought was information dressed up as entertainment. Its in-your-face style, its provocative, evocative TV journalism, made *Seven Days* the most popular current-affairs program in Canadian history. Denounced by critics for his rebellious approach, Leiterman declared, "I'm all for sensationalism, but only if it is responsible sensationalism." From 1964 to 1966, *This Hour Has Seven Days* was the talk of the country, but Watson and Leiterman were torpedoed by those who felt their sensationalism was irresponsible, and the program was cancelled by a nervous CBC management. *This Hour Has Seven Days*, however, became a model for future generations of TV journalists and was the inspiration for CBS's more subdued version, *60 Minutes*.

Sixteen years later another and more long-lasting TV journalistic experiment was led by CBC producer Mark Starowicz. *The Journal* also harnessed emotion to illuminate serious news, but it was less self-consciously provocative than *This Hour Has Seven Days*, and thanks to the interviewing skills of host Barbara Frum, it, too, became the talk of the nation. *The Journal*'s "double ender," now a standard device, was a technological breakthrough when first used by Frum to interview guests in other cities. Frum would sit in the studio staring at a blank wall while listening to her guest on an earphone and pretending to see him or her. The tape of the guest would be transmitted later to the network in Toronto and then married with the tape of Frum asking questions.

Soon after Frum's death in 1992, the program merged with *The National*. Today this prime-time hour of TV journalism, even with its damaging corner-cutting because of budget reductions, still offers some of the best produced news and current affairs in the world, rivalled only perhaps by the PBS news hour with Jim Lehrer. These programs and a few others stand out in sharp relief against the growing efforts to popularize TV news with production gimmicks, feel-good stories, and sensationalism.

Most newscasts today have turned their backs on the values

espoused by CBC News Service founder Dan McArthur, who insisted on eliminating from the news "anything in the nature of the exciting or the emotional." He opposed sensationalism in the news, rejected stories involving suicide, crime, divorce, or gambling, and worried that "showmanship creeping into the news" would elevate triviality to the status of important news.

Always there behind the scenes in commercial television was the thought that news should be a profit centre; that it should not get a free ride on the back of the profits of entertainment TV shows. Private television network and station management in Canada and the United States believed that the news should be profitable at the same time as being a program service to be displayed at CRTC and Federal Communications Commission (FCC) licence hearings to shield the fact that, as Roy Thomson once declared, a TV licence was "just like having a licence to print your own money." Local stations in North America in the 1970s and '80s began hiring experts, known as "news doctors," who advised them on how to get bigger audiences for their newscasts, allowing them to charge more for advertising. The doctors' advice essentially was to make the news more entertaining by downplaying politics, economics, international news, and anything serious and instead featuring crime, fires, accidents, and stories with happy endings. This down-market approach did indeed make the TV newsrooms profit centres, but at a cost of depriving people of some of the knowledge they need as citizens to exercise informed judgements on public issues. Ironically, the newscasts did this at the same time as newspapers were going down market to match the competition of television news.

Even though his program at times huffs and puffs at easy targets, producer Don Hewitt of CBS's *60 Minutes* worries about the increasing reliance of TV newsmagazines on sensationalist material to boost ratings. But, he says, "If you're going to compete with sitcoms, you're going to have to be entertaining." He notes the old journalistic saying that "News is news and entertainment is entertainment and never the twain shall meet." "Well," he says, "the twain have met. And it's not good."

Having discovered there was profit in news, North American stations and networks began offering not only longer, commercial-filled newscasts, but also infotainment talk shows, magazine shows, and personality shows masquerading as real news programs. These shows were not only popular, they were one-third the production cost of sitcoms or drama.

As TV newsrooms today face budget cuts and demands for bigger profits, station owners are using new technology to make do with fewer reporters and editors. The Radio-Television News Directors Association (RTNDA) says most news directors use the new technology to cut costs, "not as a way to enhance the quality of journalism." The RTNDA adds that 73 per cent of reporters in Canada and the United States say they're "uncomfortable" with using multi-skilled one-man bands, although recognizing their economic necessity. Inevitably, video-journalists, as they're called, have less time to dig out facts and their meaning because they are responsible for camera, sound, lights, and editing, as well as the editorial content itself. With their lighter, smaller, and much cheaper cameras, video-journalists are good at covering accidents and relatively uncomplicated stories. Video-journalist Nancy Durham of the CBC's London bureau says, "You can get really intimate with people, into intimate places. I don't think you could do that with a crew." However, the one-man-band approach cannot do justice to thorough coverage of city hall or national and international politics or social and economic stories.

With smaller newsroom staffs, the door more readily swings open to the subversion of the news by corporations. Corporate video news releases, for example, are often used as news without identification of their promoters. A video news release extolling the benefits of Sunlight Soap was seen in 1996 by an esitmated 7 million Canadians on newscasts on local stations. Done with high production values, the video featured Toronto's SkyDome stadium being washed and included the line "Sunlight was strong enough to do the job." All the facts and figures in the story were provided by Sunlight, although in almost all cases, the source was not reported. The washing of the stadium was an interesting story, but would have been too costly for the stations themselves to do, so editorial integrity and vigilance was lowered and a commercial product was given the status of news. The soap company got a million dollars' worth of free publicity for the $10,000 it cost to make the tape.

Producers of this kind of publicity material posing as news say they're in a partnership with the media, but, in fact, they're trying to bamboozle editors and producers, often successfully, into using a publicity gimmick for a product by pretending it's real news. It isn't.

Television news also is increasingly concerned not so much with the details of the news, but with impressions and moments that stimulate emotions rather than enrich intelligence. When I was director of news and current affairs for CBC-TV in the 1970s, my counterpart at CBS once told me, "I want their hearts; screw their minds!" Many producers use a technical bag of tricks to achieve this end. Music beds, animated graphics, stings, and other ear- and eye-grabbing devices are valuable if they're used to reinforce facts and entice viewers into examining important issues and events, but are damaging when they overwhelm the story or mislead people, as is increasingly the case. Too often the news is cheapened by production gimmicks used more to show off techniques or generate tension than to enhance understanding of a story.

The descent into superficiality by TV news, media critic Neil Postman believes, results from form triumphing over content. Canadian television's *enfant terrible*, Moses Znaimer, says that's good, as the true nature of television is about flow and process, not substance and content. While Znaimer, McLuhan, and Postman focus on the theatrical form of TV, many radio and TV journalists argue, as I do, that television news is more than a vaudeville act; that because of its enormous impact on the public, TV news must fulfil its responsibilities to inform citizens about the issues of the day, not simply pacify and entertain them. It is much harder to achieve this in private TV than in public TV, such as the CBC, PBS, or the BBC, simply because of the commercial pressures to treat viewers as consumers, not as citizens. But today, even the public systems, pushed by fear of losing audience to the private networks, sometimes flirt with being entertaining first and foremost.

Show business came to TV news back in the mid-1970s when Barbara Walters was given a million-dollar salary to co-host the ABC nightly news. Other anchors demanded equal or close to equal salaries at both the network and local big-city stations. Since then, U.S. anchor pay has zoomed. NBC's Tom Brokaw, CBS's Dan Rather, and ABC's Peter Jennings each signed up in 1997 for another five years at a reported $7 million a year. (Canadian network news anchor salaries are, at best, less than 5 per cent of that.)

To justify the higher pay cheques, more showbiz tricks were employed to grab grazing viewers and get higher ratings. Television executives judged newscasts by audience size rather than by quality. CBS's Dan Rather says the NBC nightly news moved into first place in the news ratings in late 1997 because it went soft. "News lite," he calls it. NBC News anchor Tom Brokaw, sensitive to such accusations, was indignant when NBC News signed the histrionic Geraldo Rivera for a reported $5 million a year for six years. Brokaw said that Rivera would not be allowed to appear on the Brokaw-anchored nightly news.

Alternatively, show business may have come to TV news in 1973, when Van Gordon Sauter, soon to be CBS news chief, said, "Journalism is a kind of theater." As head of CBS News, he wanted "moments" more than "facts," describing those "moments" as "a portrait of an emotional reality."

Sauter's thirst for "moments" reflects a craving to be liked rather than respected and an obsession with ratings and fear of losing to the competition of specialized news channels and, increasingly, of the Internet. In ten or fifteen years, serious news may well disappear altogether from most mainstream TV networks, except for bite-size headlines a few times a day (not dissimilar to most private radio news these days). With the networks concentrating on entertainment, TV news would go to the all-news speciality channels and the Internet until that magic day a generation or less from now when there is full convergence of the newspaper, TV, and the Internet.

For broadcasting, it's been a short and eventful life at the top. The first known broadcast news came from a station in San

Jose, California, run by the Herrold College of Engineering and Wireless in 1909, with Charles and Sybil Herrold acting as newscasters as well as disc jockeys.

Newspapers caught a whiff of the coming competition when radio carried the news of Woodrow Wilson's victory in the 1916 U.S. presidential election race hours before newspapers were on the street. Radio again beat the newspapers four years later when Warren Harding won the presidency. That same year, XWA in Montreal began regular newscasting.

In the early 1920s, the BBC began many of its newscasts with the announcer advising listeners, "It is my intention tonight to read the [news] bulletin twice, first of all rapidly and then slowly, repeating on the second occasion, when necessary, details upon which the listener may wish to take notes." The man running the BBC at the time was John Reith, a thirty-four-year-old austere intellectual who believed radio should be doing public good, not pandering to public wants with "vulgar showmanship." "To have exploited so great a scientific invention for the purpose and pursuit of entertainment alone would have been a prostitution of its powers and an insult to the character and intelligence of the public," he said. In the early days of radio, Reith insisted BBC announcers reading the news wear tuxedos as an act of courtesy for the audience and respect for the news.

That respect for journalism was also held by Guglielmo Marconi, the father of radio, who believed radio should be much more than entertainment. "Communication between peoples widely separated in space and thought is undoubtedly the greatest weapon against the evil of misunderstanding and jealousy," he said.

Thus the centuries-old newspaper battle between entertainment and education came to radio, too, as it did half a century later to television. From the beginning, however, it was clear entertainment would win the radio battle in Canada and the United States with advertisers pouring money into radio shows and personalities such as Amos 'n' Andy, Charlie McCarthy, The Happy Gang, Jack Benny, Rudy Vallee, and Wayne and Shuster.

Such newscasts as there were gave no real competition to newspapers. It was only when radio began providing on-the-spot coverage that newspapers got worried. In Canada, radio started to steal the newspapers' audience with live reports from the pithead during the Moose River, Nova Scotia, mine disaster in 1936 and stories on the birth of the Dionne Quints, the abdication of King Edward VIII (his address about "the woman I love" was carried worldwide), and stories from Germany featuring the threatening voice of Hitler. With war clouds gathering in the late 1930s, radio news got even more attention as Canadians tuned in to American newscasters Lowell Thomas, H. V. Kaltenborn, and Walter Winchell and, on the CBC, Charles Jennings and, later, Lorne Greene.

The war brought radio news to its zenith as tens of millions were transfixed by the BBC, CBC, and American network newscasts. With his "London Calling" broadcasts, complete with air-raid sirens and falling bombs crackling over the airwaves, Edward R. Murrow gave listeners a vivid sense of the war. Murrow became a household name and was almost as popular as Jack Benny, as were Murrow's "boys," such as William Shirer, Eric Severeid, Howard K. Smith, and Alexander Kendrick. In Canada, the war brought correspondents Matthew Halton, Peter Stursberg, and Marcel Ouimet into the living rooms of the nation.

After the war, the status of radio news among broadcasters declined as stations and networks with a few exceptions, such as the BBC and the CBC, turned their focus back to entertainment. Then the new kid on the block, television, came on the scene. It took a while for news on television to have any real impact, and most senior broadcast journalists initially preferred to stay on radio, believing television was too "showbizzy."

But in the 1950s, as millions of people began to turn to TV, so, too, did journalists, and soon television news leapt ahead of radio news in popularity.

Glimpses of the power of television news could be seen in 1957 during the first federal election in Canada that got full TV coverage. TV showed, as nothing else could, the grey, arrogant, staid behaviour of the Louis St. Laurent Liberals and the barnstorming evangelism of the magnetic Prairie Conservative John Diefenbaker. Television captured Diefenbaker's platform magic and, as much as anything else did, it made him the people's choice. Half a dozen years later, TV would expose Diefenbaker's self-mutilating egocentricity and his inability to delegate authority, making his political theatricality seem embarrassing rather than inspiring.

Television also made political history in the United States in 1960 when it showed the nation the charisma and intelligence of presidential candidate John F. Kennedy. The mesmerizing power of TV news was evident in the nationwide emotions that came from the 1963 TV news coverage of Kennedy's assassination and funeral, and five years later those of Robert Kennedy and Martin Luther King, Jr. The marriage of Prince Charles and Lady Diana Spencer in 1981 reached more than 2 billion people through television, and Diana's funeral sixteen years later was watched on television by an estimated 2.5 billion people, twice as many people who watched, on average, the 1996 Summer Olympics.

Television brought the Cold War into the living room as we watched history on the run during the Korean War, the Cuban Missile Crisis, the war in Vietnam. All Canada shared, through television, the last, best year of Canadian nationalism in 1967 during our one-hundredth birthday party, and it was as a result of television newscasts of the 1968 election campaign that Trudeaumania swept the country.

President Charles de Gaulle understood the power of TV news and made sure French television reflected his policies and goals, saying, "My enemies have the press, so I keep television." Closer to home, John Diefenbaker also recognized the political importance of television. One of his key aides, Gowan Guest, told me at the time, "Give us control of *The National* and give everything else to the Liberals, and we'll keep Dief in power forever!"

But the real battle for the soul of broadcast news in North America was not between opposing politicians, but between those who wanted a show and those who felt news was a public trust.

The 1970s to the 1990s were the salad days of television news, and even the most hardened, ink-stained traditionalists of the Gutenberg world had to concede, albeit reluctantly, that television news was where the action was. The stars of contemporary journalism were now the anchors and the on-air correspondents.

Television news entered a new age in 1980 with the establishment of CNN, the world's first twenty-four-hour news TV network. At the time, it was derided by some as the "Chicken Noodle Network," but today it reaches 73 million homes. A decade and a half after it began, Time-Warner took over CNN, making it the world's biggest media company with sales of $21 billion a year. In 1989, the CBC began a Canadian all-news channel. The successes of CNN and Newsworld signalled, however faintly, the end of the joyride for news on the mainstream television networks. Increasingly, the networks abdicated from providing extensive coverage of news events, leaving it to the specialized channels. That enabled networks to avoid costly pre-emptions of highly profitable entertainment programs by breaking news. Power in the networks' upper echelons began to shift to the showbiz executives who angled for more spending on entertainment and less on news. That shift may have been signalled as early as 1966 when CBS executives insisted on airing a TV rerun of the popular and profitable *I Love Lucy* instead of covering an important senate committee hearing on Vietnam. The incident led to the resignation of CBS News president Fred Friendly.

There is a striking parallel between the way newspapers lost readers to the television network newscasts and how, a couple of decades later, the networks are losing viewers to specialized channels and the Internet. There also is a parallel in the way newspapers initially discounted the impact of television and the way some TV experts of the late 1960s could not envision the narrowcasting revolution. Testifying before Senator Keith Davey's Special Senate Committee on Mass Media in 1971, the chief technical officer for Maclean Hunter Cable, Israel Switzer, said he couldn't see "things like twenty-channel systems and switch systems which use cable for access to computers. I don't feel the need for a computer in my home. . . . I think the marketability of many of these services has been dramatically overrated." They may have been overrated in 1970, but they're a reality three decades later.

As television grew, its newspaper and radio competitors changed their approach to news programming. Newspapers such as *USA Today* became more like TV in their presentation, while radio largely gave up on broadcasting news. Today, the focus of ten thousand radio stations in the United States and about five hundred in Canada is on establishing a niche identity, almost always a musical identity, although a few stations offer a non-music specialization, such as all news headlines or all talk, all religious, or all sports programming.

In the process of establishing their niches, most radio stations slashed their newscasts to on-the-hour snippets, laid off much of their news staffs, and concentrated more on presentation and comment on the news than on gathering it.

Poll after poll shows that the drop in TV network news viewing has been especially acute in the under-thirty age group. Clearly, the younger generation is the least engaged by news. One survey shows that 16 per cent of the eighteen to thirty-four age group watched U.S. TV network news in 1980, but only 6 per cent in 1995.

Broadly speaking, there are three distinct audiences for the media: the Elders, who were born between 1910 and 1945; the Baby Boomers, born between 1946 and 1964; and the Generation Xers, born after 1964. Coming right up behind the Xers is something called the "N Gen," or Net Generation, a phrase coined by Don Tapscott, Canadian author and chairman of the Alliance for Converging Technologies, to describe the newest generation enraptured by the Internet technology and beyond.

All the generations have very different news appetites: the

Elders are the biggest news consumers and the last loyal, passive viewers of TV news. The Boomers are moderate news users, and the Xers, not to mention the N Gen, are uninterested in most news. Younger people have always shown less interest in the news, but as they aged and became movers, shakers, and participants in society, their interest in news usually grew. But Generation X is different. As the Radio and Television News Directors Foundation says in a report on that generation's news habits, "They care less about what is happening in the larger world around them" than the generations before them.

As a consequence of caring less, Generation X participates less and knows less about what's happening in our political and economic life. They skim through information, getting quick hits. They're not readers, they're absorbers of visual facts, the ultimate surfers of TV and the Internet, zapping, clicking, and browsing their way across cyberspace. They are in the forefront of the computer and the Internet revolutions, and seem to focus their attention mainly on their own interests rather than society's. It is part of the Xers' and the Ns' fast-changing lives, changing jobs, friends, homes. They're more comfortable with change than Elders or Boomers and hence, for whatever news they want, since they are technologically fluent, they're more likely to go to the Internet than the traditional news sources of press, radio, and TV.

They are also more self-reliant and entrepreneurial than the Elders and Boomers. Traditional journalistic concepts of balance, objectivity, and fairness are scoffed at by the Xers and Ns, who also distrust institutions more than previous generations and are especially suspicious of politicians and the élites of industry, organizations, and the media. They want less regulation, less government, more individual rights, less moral interference.

Nobody understands this better than Toronto TV executive Moses Znaimer, himself teetering between being a young Elder and an old Boomer. The news programming on his channels is irreverent, entertainment-oriented, and fast-paced. Znaimer extols television as a triumph of the image over the printed word, and as a disciple of Marshall McLuhan, his interest is in the medium, not the message. Znaimer believes that "the best TV tells me what happened to me, today."

Producers and editors wrestling with how to reach Generation X are seeking out fast-talking and decisively derisive young faces. Their presence makes for livelier television by giving it the appearance of being cool, if not deep. Conservative American commentator Robert Novak, whose aggressive right-wing style in print and TV has been on display for years, says, "Producers want to appeal to the X Generation. They're tired of old geezers. But most of the young people don't know what they're talking about."

The danger in reaching out to the Generation Xers is that editors will cater to what they believe are their short attention spans and surface interests, turning off the more regular viewers and readers of the older generations. News could get even softer, faster, simpler, and more entertainment-focused.

As happened in the United States, Canadian network audiences began falling with the licensing of new independent stations and the arrival of cable channels. In recent years, the explosion of specialty channels has significantly eaten into national audiences. The new Canadian channels have also taken away a healthy chunk of advertising that otherwise would have gone to local TV stations and networks. Advertising on the specialty channels rose from $12 million in 1987 to $148 million in 1996 and is estimated at between $160 million to $170 million for 1997. To protect their bottom line, some TV stations developed specialty channels of their own. There are now channels devoted solely to golf or speed, history or science, food or comedy, old movies or local news or general news. In the United States, some satellite services are offering more than 250 channels, including more than three dozen movie channels, and two and a half dozen sports channels. Americans also can tune in to a BBC channel or two from the CBC.

News channels such as the CBC's Newsworld, CTV's News 1, CNN, MSNBC, Fox News, the BBC all-news channel, Euronews, several financial specialty services, and some all-local or all-regional news and information channels are also eating into the audience for network news, especially when there is a breaking news story. In Canada, audiences for the all-news channels are relatively small compared to those for network newscasts, but they rise sharply when something important is happening. The all-news channels are particularly watched by public and corporate senior management.

The all-news stations have not only changed the way we watch the news, but they also have changed the way news is gathered. Technology has made it much easier to cover breaking news stories and to cover a wider area than a single reporter could do personally. But if a reporter is covering a story by watching TV in the office and isn't on the scene, as is increasingly the case, he or she inevitably will miss the nuances, the asides, and much of the texture of an event, and won't be able to ask questions on the spot that can add depth and context to the story.

While the all-news channels offer both quick-fix news and news in depth, even more detailed coverage is available on public-affairs channels such as CPAC in Canada and C-SPAN in the

United States. Broadcasting both live and recorded events, they provide full coverage of selected events in the House of Commons and the Congress, the Supreme Court, political meetings, and significant speeches. Production values are limited, sets are sparse, and the few anchors they have are bland, but nowhere else on the dial is "the real thing" of public affairs so readily available.

Simply because they are visible, TV journalists are regarded more highly, are sought out by the public, and are better paid than their print colleagues. Some TV journalists succumb to the allure of being stars as does TV management, which publicizes them to the point that they often seem more important than the news itself. Many have become more celebrities than authorities. Indeed, some news performers seem more like graduates of drama schools than journalism schools. Good teeth, lots of hair, a nice smile, and what's called "chemistry" are often considered more important than journalism credentials. "Chemistry" is a far cry from the requirements of a good journalist, described by veteran *Toronto Star* reporter Roy Greenaway as "the hide of a dinosaur, the stamina of a Chinese coolie, the wakefulness and persistence of a mosquito, the analytical power of a detective, and the digging capacity of a steam shovel."

There used to be a saying in TV news that once you've learned to "fake sincerity," you've got it made as a successful anchor. This is a peculiarity for local stations, especially in the United States. The number of so-called "twinkie" anchors is increasing as stations try to recapture their shrinking audiences. The major Canadian networks have so far avoided most of this, but the pressure on them to replace their news anchors with more glamorous figures is increasing. News anchors and reporters, however, are journalists with an important job to do; they are in the business of informing, not performing.

Another device used to attract audience by doing something different is to move anchors out of the studios and onto the scene of a major news event. When Parliament opens or a First Ministers conference is held, Peter Mansbridge or Lloyd Robertson are on the scene. Their mere presence conveys the message that this is an important story. When the Clinton White House sex scandal hit the headlines, the anchors of the three American networks were in Cuba covering the Pope's visit. As historic and important as the Pope's trip was, the anchors were immediately ordered to fly home to be on hand for the much more entertaining story of the president's sex life. Sometimes, too, this anchor-on-the-scene approach is done solely to highlight a feature story and not to indicate its importance. News values are inevitably distorted when, wanting to boost a feature story, anchors find themselves in a wheat field or a slum just as a big story is breaking in Tokyo.

Corporate desires also sometimes influence the locale of a news program. When Disney took over ABC, the network's morning news program *Good Morning America* increased the number of shows anchored out of Disney World and Disneyland.

The "star" role for anchors is potentially dangerous because, as *Maclean's* has said, "millions of advertising dollars and even a network's integrity can depend on their images." Promoting news anchors as stars just like actors or singers encourages the idea that the news is just another part of show business. The danger is that if they are viewed only as stars, they will be chosen primarily for their looks and personality, not for their journalistic credentials.

Making stars of anchors seems also to encourage some to editorialize on stories by on-air scowling or smirking. These silent emotional displays, designed to connote support or antipathy for the words being uttered, and which some anchors apparently believe add editorial depth to a report, are especially corrosive to the anchor's necessary impartiality in reporting political news. Unlike commentators or columnists, who are supposed to have identifiable opinions in their comments, the anchor's credibility depends or his or her ability to present the news without facial editorializing. But the demands by TV stations for anchors to pay more attention to cosmetics and for editors to have more technical know-how about computers, satellites, and the Internet means that their knowledge, experience, and ethics are valued less. This, in turn, undermines the fundamental need for credible anchors, the human face of the news and the key link between the news and the public, the reliable guide through what is and is not important.

Moses Znaimer, however, says that the emphasis on image rather than content is the essence of television. What "fuelled the television revolution," he says, "can be reduced to one word: entertainment." He and many others apply that principle to all television programming, including the news, rejecting the educational role for journalism. Their stories are shorter, faster-paced, and carry as many jolts per minute as possible, a style copied from high-energy, quick-cut commercials. They make liberal use of teasers and bumpers about what's coming up next, dramatic musical stings, and encourage the anchors to chit chat between news items and commercials. These devices, soft news features, and the advertisements themselves have reduced a thirty-minute newscast on commercial stations in North America to about twelve minutes of hard news – enough to fill about half to three-quarters of the front page of most newspapers. When he first began anchoring CBS-TV news, Walter Cronkite suggested he end the newscasts each night by saying, "For more information, read your local newspaper." His bosses said no because they didn't want to admit to the brevity of TV news, nor did they want to help a competitor. Cronkite's sign-off became "And that's the way it is," which was to say, that was all the news that could be fitted into the network's news time.

When television became the dominant medium for the dissemination of news, it fundamentally changed the dynamics of politics. Campaigns started to be shaped for what would be seen on the evening news. Photo opportunities, not the substance of party policy, were what really mattered. The last U.S. presidential election saw political parties raise more than $800 million for campaign expenses, according to the Federal Communications Commission (FCC), most of it going to TV advertising.

To a large degree, television has taken politics out of the church basements, auditoriums, arenas, and picnic grounds and transferred it to the television screen. In the process, politics has become more visible, but, simultaneously and incongruously, less participatory and less substantive. A TV debate by prime ministerial and presidential candidates is seen by the media and by the politicians as a beauty contest more than an articulation of policy issues. When a federal budget is handed down in Ottawa, the government and opposition spokespeople concentrate not on a detailed response to reporters' questions, but on delivering a socko ten-second clip that will get repeated in TV newscasts. Getting on television news has become the central objective of politicians.

To try to break out from image-focused politics, some networks, such as the CBC, have assigned senior correspondents to report only on issues, much to the chagrin of the political parties. Exploring issues is viewed suspiciously by party officials, who prefer the more controllable image politics.

My first awareness of the impact of television in politics came while I was following the presidential campaign of Dwight Eisenhower in 1952. He never did like TV. He became wooden and unsure under its bright lights, and once, when his teleprompter suddenly stopped in the middle of a live address to the nation, he, too, stopped. Although the silence lasted less than a minute, it seemed an agonizing age and then Ike bristled to the watching nation, "The goddamn thing's stopped!" He waited some more and then it started, and on he went with his speech.

The teleprompter may have been a challenge for Ike, but it has been invaluable both for politicians and for anchors. It meant that they could seem to be speaking directly to the audience while, in fact, they were simply reading off a script projected before them on the camera lens. Many a time as an anchor, my teleprompter stopped or even started to run backwards, but fortunately, unlike Eisenhower, I always had a spare script in front of me so I could carry on.

In the early days of TV news, there was no such thing as a teleprompter; the anchors simply read their scripts head down with little eye contact with the audience. In an attempt to create more of a relationship between anchor and audience, one early TV producer, Don Hewitt, the veteran CBS producer of *60 Minutes*, tried to get the CBS News anchor of the time, Douglas

Edwards, to learn Braille so that he could do the newscast with his fingers flicking across the pages in front of him while he looked directly into the camera. Edwards, however, couldn't learn Braille and resorted to printing out the newscast in large letters on long cardboard sheets that would be held up just at the side of the camera lens. It was a technique used widely by anchors and politicians before the "prompter" came to the rescue, at last giving the anchor full eye contact with the viewers.

Dwight Eisenhower was the first U.S. president to allow TV cameras to regularly record his news conferences. Ike's advisers, however, perhaps remembering the teleprompter incident, wouldn't allow live coverage. That didn't happen until John F. Kennedy became president. The political power of television was first widely seen in the United States during Kennedy's 1960 victory over Richard Nixon. The most compelling television images I recall from the campaign were those of the "squealers" and the "jumpers," exuberant young women, sometimes including nuns, who screamed and leapt whenever Kennedy appeared and whose ardour was captured by the TV news cameras.

Kennedy understood the political power of TV, not only in showing the enthusiasm of his supporters, but in conveying the sense of competence and confidence that he exuded, especially during the TV debate with Nixon, which, arguably, won him the presidency. Within a week of entering office, Kennedy held the first live, televised presidential news conference and demonstrated his domination of the TV camera. As I sat there among my colleagues listening to him, I marvelled at his deft handling of questions about Khrushchev, Laos, the Congo, and domestic issues. He used the camera to woo the 60 million Americans watching with his assurance, quickness, knowledge, and self-deprecatory wit. He knew not only what to say and how to say it for the best effect on TV, but also how to dress for television, how to use the lights, and what gestures and camera angles were most effective. His press secretary, Pierre Salinger, later told me that after every TV news conference, he would critique his own performance, saying, "I could have done better on that" or "That camera angle murders me!"

Kennedy felt at home in front of the camera and he had the added advantage of liking most reporters since he'd been a reporter himself. In a conversation on a campaign swing, he once told me how much he'd loved reporting for the Hearst papers on the founding of the United Nations in San Francisco in 1945 and, that same year, reporting on Sir Winston Churchill's election defeat. "After I'm through with politics," he smiled, "I might become a newspaper editor or publisher!"

In the decades after Kennedy, however, television began to sour on politics because producers felt the public was bored by it. At the 1996 U.S. Presidential Nominating Convention, the American TV networks offered gavel-to-gavel coverage on their specialty channels or Internet Web sites to buttress their abbreviated nightly on-air convention coverage. It was a message of the future. With the growing number of news speciality channels and with about half of the homes in the United States expected to be on-line by the year 2000 or shortly thereafter, and with Canada not far behind, the future of news lies with the new technology, not the old.

8

The New Deity

"**E**lectricity will take the place of God," Vladimir Lenin told a colleague in 1918. As the children of an electrical era, we are opening the door to the third age of the last millennium. We have gone from the Agricultural Age spearheaded by a man behind a horse and plough, to the Industrial Age led by machines, and to the Information Age with computers guiding the way. With electricity as its fuel, the new technology has the potential for unlimited worldwide communications or, if misused, catastrophic global dysfunction.

The revolutionary digital communications technology constitutes a new deity, a great conveyor belt in the sky providing a dizzying diversity of information that can be transmitted in any combination of video, audio, or text infinitely faster than ever before. The equivalent of the entire Manhattan telephone book, for instance, could be transmitted to your modem in three seconds. A new, ultra-fast system is now being developed that will transmit the contents of all thirty volumes of the *Encyclopaedia Britannica* in one second. Digital and Internet technology have put the world literally at our fingertips, and we have far easier access to data banks around the globe than ever before. However, these informational riches are available only to the "haves" of the world; many among the "have-nots" of the Third World have never even made a telephone call.

Digital technology, says Wade Rowland, one of Canada's most respected technology writers and a one-time CBC news executive, "may be the most important development in the entire history of communications technologies."

Digital technology – by, in effect, enlarging the pipeline that delivers data to your home or office – is poised to bring knock-your-socks-off-quality pictures to your TV as well as being used to expand the number of channels it can receive. It will be able to squeeze four, six, or more (some broadcasters say twelve) standard quality channels into the space used by one high-quality channel. The original idea of digital transmission was to give viewers a much sharper picture, but TV executives, worried that the public won't pay the high price for a new, improved TV set just for better-quality pictures, are attracted to using digital technology not so much for quality as for quantity. With some of the new channels being pay channels and others generating more advertising, broadcasters could get new revenue streams, which, among other things, would help them pay the $1 million or $2 million cost per station for the new digital equipment as well as fattening their bottom lines. A station could offer a combination of a few high-quality programs during prime time and then at other times use digital to provide additional standard-quality channels.

The U.S. government wants the country's 1,600 TV stations to go digital by 2006. It hopes that a dozen stations in ten cities will start digital transmissions in November 1998, 40 more stations by the spring of 1999, and an additional 120 stations by November 1999. At that point, more than half of U.S. viewers would be served by digital; seven years later, all stations would be digital. Canada likely will be a year or two behind. It is hoped that there will be digital TV in Toronto, Vancouver, and Montreal in 1999, and by 2007 all Canadian stations may be digital. That timetable may slip, however, because of the economic and hardware hurdles yet to be crossed. Some suggest it may be 2010 or so before the entire Canadian system is digital. Until then, TV stations will be able to broadcast using their old technology as well as digital, on the assumption that TV viewers need the time between now and then to replace their present sets. While new broadcasting equipment will be expensive for station and network owners, the big money in digital in the near future is what you and I will have to spend for new, digital TV sets. In 1998, a digital TV costs $1,500 to $2,000 more than an analog set. In five years, that price likely will be down to around $500 more, and in ten years, only $200 to $300 more. That adds up: in Canada there are about 20 million sets to be replaced, and about 240 million in the United States.

Digital TV holds significant implications for the news. It opens a whole new world of special effects, graphics, and animation, which, depending on how they're used, could trivialize the news even more, or offer more depth, or, curiously, even do both. It's unlikely TV networks and stations will use digital technology to improve picture sharpness for the news since a high-definition shot of a politician at a news conference is not going to excite viewers or editors. More likely the extra channel space will allow innovations, particularly on the all-news specialty channels, including the ability for you to get supplementary information. On a split screen, you could click on one part of the screen to get the full text of what was said, or get background information on a news personality either in text or video, or you could leave the main channel and tune into a sub-channel providing the background.

There also could be closer tie-ins between news and commercial sales. For instance, if you're watching an interview with an author, you might click on a sales order form at the corner of the screen to buy a copy of the book under discussion. The station would get a percentage of the sale from the publisher as a bookstore now does. The danger, of course, is that the station might, in time, become more interested in selling merchandise and distort the program to meet that objective.

A new stage in technology is the much talked about convergence of the Internet and your TV screen. With this, you no longer need a computer to access the Internet. All you need is a small box sitting atop the TV set that brings many of the wonders of the World Wide Web onto your screen. Without a keyboard, it is less participatory than the regular Internet, but it allows split screen, with TV on one side and the Internet on the other. By touching the screen or using a remote-control device, it is possible to get more detail on a subject or to place orders for goods and services. With a keyboard, it also can be used to send e-mail, freeing people from what Internet users call the "snail mail" of regular post office delivery. The cost of the convergence box – about $300 – would be significantly less than a computer and provides a lean-back approach to viewing the Internet, unlike the lean-forward style of using a computer.

When these technical innovations happen, the news business will change dramatically. Whether on television, in print, on the Internet, or on some yet-to-be-developed medium, news companies likely will offer many different formats of news, just as General Motors has many different models of cars for different needs and desires. For instance, a digitalized channel could offer three or four different newscasts at the same time, each tailored for a specific region, much as newspapers are doing with their differing regional editions.

The Internet, says Wade Rowland, is "intrinsically favourable to the advancement of democracy." He adds that, "It is a world that finds beauty, meaning, order and life in chaos. It suggests a civilization that promotes and values diversity, even anarchy. It suggests a politics that values individualism above corporatism; connectivity above collectivity; nimbleness above persistence; honour above duty."

Clearly, the Internet will have a dramatic impact on the news: on how it's delivered, who produces it, what its content is, what its ethics are. It has the capacity to be socially destructive or socially constructive, depending on how we use it.

It all began with computers built to meet the military's needs for fast calculations during the Second World War, although the idea itself had been conceived by Charles Babbage in the mid-1800s. The world's first working computer, the IBM Automatic Sequence Calculator, Mach I, began operating in 1942, at Harvard University. A year later, the British developed a computer for fast decoding of the German cypher system. Shortly after the war, IBM developed the Electronic Numerical Integrator and Computer (ENIAC), the fastest computer in the world at the time, which occupied eighteen hundred square feet of floor space and weighed thirty tons. By 1951, the first commercial computer was developed. Called UNIVAC – Universal Automatic Computer – it could work ten times faster than ENIAC.

The first major journalistic use of the computer was in the

1952 U.S. presidential election, when CBS used UNIVAC to calculate the election results. At the time, it was thought that only a few computers were needed in any one country. Much of the development of computers was spurred by the military's Cold War needs, and by the 1960s, smaller computers, costing $15,000 to $20,000 each, were being produced for business and industry. In 1975, there was serious talk of the possibility of personal computers. At that point, computers began to take off as a playground for scientists and techno-wizards and a launching pad for the Internet. Today, there are tens of millions of computers around the world.

The Internet is now long past its swaddling clothes, but is still relatively young, having been born in 1969 as a Pentagon network called ARPANET. It was designed to provide decentralized computer communications among the U.S. military, researchers, and Defence contractors and to protect information and keep it flowing in the event of a nuclear attack. When the U.S. government stopped funding ARPANET in 1989, its private users carried on, launching the cybernetic information age.

The dynamic spread of the Internet in the United States can be seen when compared to newspapers. It took one hundred years before newspapers reached a 50 per cent penetration of the population. The Internet will do it in ten or fifteen years, most experts forecast.

The U.S. Commerce Department says that more than 100 million people were on-line around the world by the end of 1997. By 2001, the number will reach an estimated 268 million, according to the U.S. research company Data Quest. Another researcher, International Data Corporation (IDC), forecasts that Internet users by the year 2000 will number 550 million. Whatever the specific number, clearly in the first half of the twenty-first century, the Internet's impact on society likely will equal that of the automobile, telephone, and perhaps even electricity itself.

For many, the Internet has become an obsession with its endless research capabilities, e-mail, and chat groups. "Cyberhooked" users stare at their screens for hours. It's estimated there are more than 8.1 million cyber addicts in the United States alone, spending sixty to eighty hours a week on-line, neglecting food, family, and sleep. It's true in Canada as well, where a government-sponsored survey showed many Canadians feel Internet surfing can be hazardous to family life. A Florida woman in late 1997 lost custody of her two children when a judge ruled she was so addicted to the Internet that she had neglected them. In several U.S. states, including Florida, Internet support groups have been established for the cyberhooked, and the University of Pittsburgh has set up a Center for Online Addiction.

The popularity of the Internet is shown in the increasing number of on-line commercial transactions. The U.S. Commerce Department says 10 million people in the United States and Canada made Internet purchases in 1997. In 1996, according to researchers at Jupiter Communications, Internet purchases totalled about $700 million and in 1997 are estimated at $2.6 billion. Most American retailers expect sales on the Web to account for more than 20 per cent of their business within three to five years.

But the most dramatic figures are in business-to-business transactions on the Internet. Forrester Research calculates that such business deals on the Web in 1997 reached $8 billion in 1997, ten times the figure for the previous year, and in mid-1998 the U.S. government forecast such transactions would reach $300 billion by 2002.

A big attraction of the Internet is that selling costs are low.

A Booz-Allen & Hamilton research report says a basic over-the-counter transaction costs $1.07 to process while the cost is about one cent on the Internet. The normal cost to process an airline ticket is estimated at $10.50, but on the Internet it can be done for about $1.50. Canadian banking industry figures show a cost of four cents per Internet transaction compared to fifteen cents at an automated banking machine and $1.50 at a teller's cage.

When a bomb blew up a federal building in Oklahoma City in April 1995, the Internet scooped even CNN. People on the street rushed to their computers to post detailed accounts of the explosion on their Web sites. Much of it was inaccurate, but it reflected a need to communicate the horror of what they'd witnessed. The crash of a Boeing 747 in Guam in mid-1997 was reported first on the Internet on the AP Web site and seven minutes later on the AP regular wire. The death of Princess Diana was a defining moment for the Internet. Millions followed the story and discussed her fatal accident and funeral on the Internet. More than one hundred Diana Web sites sprang up after the accident, offering details, background, and discussion on her death as people both sought more information from alternative sources beside the regular media and also wanted to share their feelings about her with others. Nothing like it had ever happened before. CNN's Web site got nearly 60 million "hits" from Internet users, substantially more than the 45 million "hits" that the NASA Web site received on the Mars Pathfinder mission.

During his trial in Los Angeles, there were Web sites on O. J. Simpson scattered across the Internet landscape, awash in gossip, speculation, and discussion about his wife's murder. Within days of JonBenet Ramsey's murder in Boulder, Colorado, her parents had set up a Web site of their own to tell their version of the tragedy.

Far-right-wing militia groups and rabble-rousing racists, such as neo-Nazi Ernst Zundel in Toronto, thrive on the Internet, nourished by their own paranoid Web site warnings of United Nations troops invading the country in black helicopters, dismissing the Holocaust, and seeing communists and traitors behind every lamppost.

It is in politics, however, that the Internet displays most vividly its richness and its dangers. It offers journalists immense depth of background data, voting records, policies, and personal information. Increasingly, journalists and political junkies are cruising the Internet to find out what's happening and why. Politicians are unable to hide their past when any reporter can get their life story at the click of a mouse. They have countered with their own Web sites, putting their twist on events and issues. Political parties have Web sites where they lay out their perceptions of the nation's challenges. On the Internet, politicians, "spin doctors," and other advocates can take their views directly to the public, bypassing journalists altogether with their own news programs and stories.

The problem is that this kind of information inevitably mixes fact and fancy to fit a particular agenda. The news these sites offer is not subject to the standards of professional journalism. As anybody can set up a Web site offering his or her opinions on anything, there is a superabundance of factually suspect advocacy journalism. News consumers simply don't have the time and patience to digest and evaluate all the news on the Internet. Clearly, the more sources there are, the more the public will need brand-name journalists to offer a reliable pathway through the forest of news. For instance, at the height of the hepatitis C controversy in Canada, via the search engine infoseek you could get information from 5,896 Web pages, offering medical details and personal stories.

The Internet is a battleground for the guerrillas and the gorillas; the hit-and-run amateurs and the brand-name professionals. Back when television began to replace newspapers as the principal source of news, TV took over as *the* medium of politics. At first, the main networks carried full or almost full coverage of political conventions, of campaigns, and of election night. But after specialized news channels such as CNN and Newsworld came along, the main networks began reducing their coverage and their audience dropped. This was seen in the U.S. presidential debates on the networks, which drew an average TV audience of 41.2 million in 1996 compared to 68.4 million in 1992. With network audiences declining, viewers of the all-news channels sharply increased as they gave blanket coverage from the early days of the campaign to election night. The 1996 U.S. presidential election, however, also saw the arrival of a new rival, the Internet, which suddenly became a major political player, providing even more coverage than the news channels.

The Web site of the *New York Times*, for instance, provided full texts of all the significant campaign news conferences, along with hundreds of pages of background information. If you entered your Zip code, you could get the full voting records of your local representative. On election night, you also could get information on how each county voted. Some Web sites had more than ten thousand pages of political information, so much that no one editor could know everything that was on the site. On the first of the presidential debates, CBS anchor

Dan Rather announced the CBS Web site address and within a few minutes the site got more than a million hits, so many that the whole system broke down under the volume of the demand.

The Freedom Forum Foundation estimates that 28 per cent of U.S. voters were on-line at some point during the 1996 campaign, and election night saw millions of Internet hits from people seeking results. Inevitably, this drew audiences away from the main networks. On election night, the four U.S. networks – NBC, CBS, ABC, and CNN – had a combined audience rating of 25.4 per cent compared to 39.4 per cent in the previous presidential election.

Although its coverage was not as extensive as during the U.S. campaign, the Internet was also a player in the last Canadian federal election. The parties flexed muscles on their own Web sites and networks offered background material on theirs. Special-interest groups spun the issues according to their perspectives, and discussion groups and individuals offered personal opinions. In Quebec, separatists established a Web site to ridicule Prime Minister Jean Chrétien and the Queen. Chrétien was shown wearing clown make-up that exaggerated the partial paralysis of his mouth, while the Queen's head was stuck on a cow. The next federal election will see the Internet playing a much bigger role.

The era of news coming only from a daily newspaper or a once-a-day network TV news program has disappeared. The papers and the networks are now providing news packages to different news distributors and increasingly to the Internet.

The question is who will win the competition for news primacy on the Internet: the networks, the newspapers, or the cowboys who have little journalistic background but have immense enthusiasm for the freedom of the Internet? If we are going to have a society more aware of itself, the answer has to be brand-name professional journalists who offer news as education and illumination more than as entertainment. Newspapers have the advantage in this because of their far greater resources. Television, however, has the advantage of picture expertise. The Radio and Television News Directors Foundation notes in a study on the future, "When it takes just a few seconds to download a full-motion video news clip on the Internet, TV newsrooms will gain the edge over their print counterparts." Maybe so, but editorial depth has to go with the pictures, and that is more likely found in newspaper companies than in most TV newsrooms.

Inevitably, the future will see a growing number of partnerships between newspapers and TV stations and networks to maximize the benefits for news distribution on the Internet. Brand-name news providers must also provide an outlet for at least some of the free-wheeling discussions and opinionated amateurs. But the heart of any future journalism, whether in print, on the air, or on the Internet, lies in the quality of those providing the news. "The advances in technology will require journalists to do more critical analysis, more in-depth stories," says Henry Ingle at the University of Texas in El Paso. "It will require them to go deeper into their stories. As a result, journalism and journalists will become much more important."

9

So . . . What to Do?

As it has been from the beginning, the central issue for journalism today, no matter the technology, is whether news is for education or for entertainment. In reality, it has to be a mix of both, but with a clear emphasis on the former. The focus of the media's microscopes and telescopes must be on educating in as popular a manner as possible without distorting reality. Energizing brain cells is more important than zapping corneas.

The future of democracy rests on the quality of the political, economic, and social decisions that are made by the public and its leaders. Those decisions are based on citizen attitudes shaped by what knowledge they get from the news media. News is thus a necessity in the advancement of civilization. The role of journalists, as the Toronto *Telegram* described it in 1889, is to be "the lungs of civilization." The news media's function, in reflecting the important issues facing society, is to provide full and accurate reportage of facts, context, and background, and to offer various shades of opinion based on those facts. In short, to report both on what's happening and what it means.

Pioneer Canadian journalism professor Wilfrid Eggleston once wrote, "Survival of all living creatures requires an awareness of the changing environment. . . . Accurate information is required for people to react." But the full range of accurate information has been diminished in the pursuit of trivia. President Clinton's sex life, O. J. Simpson's trials, or Princess Diana's life and death titillate our imaginations, but don't educate our minds, and furthermore the overwhelming coverage crowds out the politically, economically, and socially important stories. It's a dumbing down of the news that in turn lowers the quality of public knowledge and undermines the quality of public decision-making. In the process of down-marketing, traditional standards that have given credibility to the media for decades have been thrust aside by many news organizations in hot pursuit of scandal and catastrophe, weakening public respect for the media.

There are three groups responsible for the quality of news: the public, journalists, and news organizations.

A public that indulges primarily in tragedy, calamity, oddity, conflict, and sex is a public unprepared for intelligent discourse on major issues and knowledgeable decision-making. It is also a public whose participation in the processes of democracy is woefully inadequate, as recent voting statistics graphically demonstrate.

It is too easy to put all the blame on the media. The public itself has to share the blame for citizen apathy for it, too, has responsibilities in a democracy, as well as rights. People have a right to high-quality journalism, but they also have a responsibility to demand a journalism that prepares them to make informed judgements so that they can be participants rather than passive observers in local, regional, and national debates.

It's not good enough for people to just shout out in frustration against the media à la Paddy Chayefsky's movie *Network*, saying that they're "not going to take it any more." They must initiate a dialogue with the media about their needs as well as their wants. Unpalatable as it may seem to some, a participatory democratic society is a schoolroom and journalists are its teachers. There are many other sources of knowledge of current events, of course, but for most people, journalism is the most readily available.

Although many journalists are hesitant about the idea, the public must be a creative partner of the media in stimulating quality journalism. A few years ago, a number of news organizations appointed ombudsmen who would investigate public complaints about news stories. It was a good idea, but recent budget-cutting has eliminated most of them in the United States and Canada. In Canada, for instance, only the *Toronto Star*, the Halifax *Chronicle-Herald*, and the CBC have official ombudsmen. In the United States with fifteen hundred newspapers, there are about forty ombudsmen. In Europe, however, there is a rising interest in the ombudsman function with, for example, recent appointments in French television and at the influential Paris newspaper *Le Monde*.

Another useful approach tried by the CBC and BBC was the formation of citizen advisory councils on various subjects, such as religion, science, and agriculture. For years at the CBC, these councils met two or three times a year with journalism programming executives and producers, and as director of news and current affairs for the CBC at the time, I found them an invaluable, even if occasionally critical, source of program evaluation and ideas. Sadly, as a result of Ottawa's cuts to the CBC's budget, these advisory councils were allowed to lapse.

A further route for public involvement with the media is the news councils and press councils set up by the media in provinces across Canada. They provide the public with another place for concerns to be expressed about media coverage. In addition to ombudsmen and news councils, a process also should be in place for redress of errors or unfairness, including an "Our Mistake" section for corrections.

An increasing number of newspapers are seeking to get in closer touch with their local communities by providing a forum for public debate, and more fully reporting on citizen concerns. Although not much has been done on this in Canada as yet, the Freedom Forum Foundation in the United States is spending $1 million to encourage this approach, and at least three other U.S. journalistic organizations are conducting studies and projects on responsible journalism.

The approach, called "public journalism," remains controversial among some news people, though, because it alters the role of news organizations from reflecting to stimulating community activity. The focus on "public journalism," however, is a refreshing indication that at least some news organizations feel they don't have to go down market and that they have a responsibility to stimulate citizen interest in public issues.

Whatever form it takes, a greater public participation in encouraging quality journalism is essential for the credibility of the media and for the vibrancy of our democracy. Socially responsible journalism does not mean total reliance on focus groups or an abdication of editorial responsibility for editors and reporters. But it does mean a more intense examination of the news that's important.

There has been some reluctance by many senior media executives to let the public have a role – any role – in journalistic decision-making. Their argument is that journalists know best.

But we don't. Socially responsible, professionally skilled, and knowledgeable news media know a lot, but not enough. We can always benefit from public input.

In effect, the news media provide a marketplace for the sellers of ideas: the politicians, social activists, business and labour leaders. To my mind, the media's loyalty lies first of all with the buyers – the public – not the sellers. The media are, in effect, an agent for the public in providing that marketplace of information on what's happening, where, when, why, and how.

In achieving reliable, respected journalism, all news organizations should have a written code of policies and standards, and an internal process for articulating, applying, and monitoring those policies and standards. The code should be given to every reporter and editor, and also given to the public so that they can measure policies against practices. Newspaper and broadcasting industry codes, as well as some for individual news organizations such as Canadian Press or the CBC, already exist, but few have any system for regular review.

Among the needs for respected journalism is a distinct separation between opinion journalism and factual reportage so that news stories are not contaminated by opinions. A balanced presentation of point-of-view commentaries is essential, but so, too, is reportage untainted by reportorial bias.

Better hiring practices are needed, too, as is improved training at the beginning and during staff careers. The role of schools of journalism is critical in preparing would-be journalists in both the theory and the practice of news. They need to work closely with news organizations to emphasize the values of quality news and to enrich each other – the media providing lecturers on the day-to-day realities of journalism and the professors relating those realities to purpose, policy, and standards.

More foreign correspondents based in the news hot spots around the world and greater use of their material would improve and deepen the coverage of international issues. So would the hiring of more specialized reporters to provide explanation and enlightenment on events and issues in fields such as economics, science, education, arts, business, labour, and the environment, among other areas.

The basic job of a journalist is not necessarily to please anybody, with the possible exception of Diogenes, waving his lamp and looking for an honest man. We're not here primarily to please or entertain politicians, business or labour leaders, social activists, or other "spinners" of news seeking public support. We have to recognize that as long as journalists are doing a professionally and socially responsible job as agents for the public, there will be, and there should be, a continuing tension – often tempestuous, sometimes ferocious, but never-ending – between the media and the news makers, who are selling their own agendas and versions of the truth.

The journalists' role is to inform, to explain, to provide context and background, to look to the future, to stimulate interest in public affairs, to review various points of view on issues, actions, and events, to reflect social cooperation as well as confrontation. Journalists send signals to society in their factual news coverage, and in editorials and commentaries they evaluate those signals.

It is also the responsibility of news organizations to provide overall balance and comprehensiveness in their reports. That means covering the widest possible range of views and taking into account the weight of opinion holding those views. The greater emphasis obviously goes to the views held by the most people. But challenges to the establishment and to accepted orthodoxies must be reported, too, since an important function of the media is to alert society to alternative views and to options for change.

The news media are not simply spectators at issues and events. We journalists are participants because we identify those issues and events for others. We choose the ones we consider significant and set others aside. We hold a mirror up to society, but we do so selectively. We have to recognize that the simple act of raising that mirror changes the character of the event or issue by intensifying, glamorizing, or denigrating it. We must be as sure as we can that we are giving a fair reflection of reality and truth when we raise that mirror.

We're not giving truth a fair chance if we are adversaries in our news stories, if we sensationalize, if we're lazy or careless or unscrupulous, if we're shallow or simplistically looking only for good guys and bad guys. We must look not only for the obvious, but for the nuances and subtleties of complex situations.

The most important quality in the media today is fairness. This may be optional for news "spinners" and supermarket tabloids, but it is a necessity for journalists. That means being fair to both the big and the small, to the likeable and the unlikeable.

Reporters and editors, in both the stories and the headlines over their stories, must attempt to provide untainted news so the public can make up its own mind. In some ways, we journalists must have the same attitude towards news as an employee of a bank has towards money – it isn't ours. We're handling it on behalf of other people so we cannot put it to our own use. If we do, it's embezzlement.

Part of being fair is making judgements on when the public's right to know conflicts with the equally fundamental right in a democracy of privacy and a fair trial. There is no clear-cut formula for when the right to know does and does not override the right to privacy, except that it does so, in my judgement, rarely.

It does so if evidence of abuse of power is uncovered. It does so if a reporter finds that the private behaviour of a public official endangers the performance of his or her public duties. It does so if the personal history of a public official is important and relevant. And it does so in serious investigative reportage into criminal activities.

These and perhaps a few other circumstances are exceptions to a general rule that the right of privacy is supreme. The media have no divine right to prowl recklessly through the private lives of citizens on journalistic fishing expeditions.

One reason for public distaste for journalism is the growing sense that reporters and editors are a cynical lot who have lost all faith in the world. H. L. Mencken, the iconoclastic Baltimore writer, once called his fellow reporters and editors "the human character in disintegration." That's a little harsh, but cynicism is a word that applies too often these days to reporters. I believe we must develop a healthy scepticism, but never cynicism.

In establishing ethics, standards, and priorities, news organizations set the tone of their journalism, which ranges wildly in Canada from the CBC to Moses Znaimer's stations, from the *Globe and Mail* to the *Toronto Sun*. But while news companies establish the temperament of their coverage, it is the editors and reporters who are responsible for implementing it. They are the front-line combatants in the journalistic wars. As we try to keep the record straight and expose those who fiddle with the truth, we may seem to be a nosy and cheeky bunch, but our role is to point a searchlight and probe through the confusing, complicated avalanche of news. We may just report history on the run, and imperfectly at that, but responsible journalism can bring all of us as close to the truth as we'll ever get for a long time. It's our job in news to keep trying to improve our journalism, this imperfect necessity, and be better agents for the public in reporting what's going on.

Reporting the news fairly and fearlessly is critical for a democratic society and fulfilling for the journalist. As I write, in my head are echoing the words I heard at a long-ago lunch with a group of Washington correspondents listening to Walter Lippmann speak about the role of journalists. "We perform an essential service," he said. "It is no mean calling and we have a right to be proud of it, to be glad it is our work."

I am. But we must never cease to make it better.

Acknowledgements

There are many people I should thank for their help over the years, but especially for this book, I owe a deep debt of gratitude to my editor at McClelland & Stewart, Dinah Forbes, whose assistance in shaping and clarifying the manuscript was outstanding. Thanks, too, to Heather Sangster, who, as my copy editor, made grammatical sense out of the manuscript as well as correcting my misadventures in spelling, punctuation, and repetition.

My CBC colleague Jim Littleton provided invaluable counsel on the manuscript. In researching the book, I was also aided substantially by numerous authorities at the Freedom Forum Foundation, particularly Larry McGill and his colleagues at the foundation's Media Studies Center in New York, by Adam Powell in Washington, D.C., and by the authorities at the Newseum in Arlington, Virginia. The Radio and Television News Directors Foundation, including project director Mark Thalhimer, was especially helpful in providing background material, as was the Pew Research Center for the People and the Press in Washington, the Los Angeles Times Mirror Center for the People and the Press, and the Newspaper Association of America. Also of great value for my research was the Canadian Newspaper Association, especially its former president, Richard Dicerni, and research director, Charles Dunbar. I must also thank the CBC engineering department and, for his specialized knowledge and insight, Professor Derrick de Kerckhove, director of the University of Toronto's McLuhan Program in Culture and Technology. Anne Mercer of the CBC Reference Library in Toronto was also very helpful in steering me to valuable reference material.

As she has so many times before, my wife, Lorraine Thomson, laboured with me through the preparation of the manuscript providing invaluable advice and guidance and being wondrously patient. So was our family: Fred and Francesca Parker and, with the special insight of the young, our grandchildren, Jesse and Robert Parker.

To all of the above and a great many others, I owe much, both for this book and for the pleasures and riches of the journalistic journey I have taken since the mid-1940s.

Index

Rothschild, Nathan, 79
Rowe, Sandra Mims, 23, 168
Rowland, Wade, 73, 90, 207, 210
Royal Canadian Air Farce, 134
Rusk, Dean, 129
Russell, William Howard, 124

Sackett, Lawrence, 148
Safer, Morley, 112, 130
St. John, Robert, 126
St. Laurent, Louis, 192
St. Petersburg Times, 12, 169
Salinger, Pierre, 205
Salisbury, Lord, 85
Santayana, George, 107
Sarah, Duchess of York, 162
Saturday Evening Post, 30
Sauter, Van Gordon, 189
Sawyer, Diane, 18-19
Scott, C. P., 32, 103
Second World War, 126
Seinfeld, 97
Seldes, Gilbert, 182-83
Severeid, Eric, 180, 191
Shaw, George Bernard, 52, 107
Shirer, William, 191
Shuster, Frank, 191
Sifton, Sir Clifford, 141
Simpson, Nicole, 160
Simpson, O. J., 10, 24, 37, 41, 49, 52, 100, 160, 213, 219
Sinclair, Gordon, 102, 143
Singleton, Dean, 147, 166
60 Minutes, 112, 184-85, 203
Sky TV Services, 47

Smathers, George, 62
Smith, Goldwin, 123
Smith, Howard K., 191
Socrates, 74
Sophocles, 115
Southam Inc., 153-54, 174
Southam, William, 141
Spanish Civil War, 126
Spanish–American War, 88
Spencer, Earl, 162
Spencer, Herbert, 130
Sports Illustrated, 30
Springer, Jerry, 39
Spry, Graham, 54
Stalin, Joseph, 55, 133
Stanley, Henry Morton, 87
Stanton, Frank, 130
Star (U.K. tabloid), 159
Star (U.S. tabloid), 71, 163
Star TV Services, 47
Starowicz, Mark, 184
StarPhoenix (Saskatoon), 154
Stead, W. T., 16
Steffens, Lincoln, 89-90, 107
Stephens, Mitchell, 70-71, 78, 92
Stern, Howard, 38-39, 172
Stone, I. F., 114
Storey, William, 125
Stursberg, Peter, 191
Sukarno, 65
Sun (London), 13, 20, 31, 98, 100, 159, 162-63
Sun (New York), 84, 87
Sun Media, 99, 153, 164, 174
Sun Tzu, 124